WISDOM
DECLARATIONS
With the Book of Proverbs

TAMI MILLER

urbanpress

Wisdom Declarations
by Tami Miller
Copyright ©2023 Tami Miller

ISBN #978-1-63360-241-0

Unless otherwise identified, Scripture quotations are taken from The Passion Translation®, a registered trademark of Passion & Fire Ministries, Inc. Copyright © 2020 Passion & Fire Ministries, Inc.

Scripture quotations marked NIV are taken from THE HOLY BIBLE: New International Version ©1978 by the New York International Bible Society, used by permission of Zondervan Bible Publishers. All rights reserved.

Scripture quotations marked NKJV are taken from the New King James Version®. Copyright© 1982 by Thomas Nelson, Inc. Used by permission. All rights reserved.

Scripture quotations marked NLT are taken from the Holy Bible, New Living Translation, copyright © 1996, 2004, 2015 by Tyndale House Foundation. Used by permission of Tyndale House Publishers, Inc., Carol Stream, Illinois 60188. All rights reserved.

For Worldwide Distribution   Printed in the U.S.A.

Urban Press
P.O. Box 8881
Pittsburgh, PA 15221-0881 USA
412.646.2780
www.urbanpress.us

Dedication

This project is dedicated to my beautiful, classy Mom, Dolores Ferguson. Thank you for teaching me all the things, especially this one that helps me with all the other ones. Your legacy lives on.

Introduction

I grew up as a preacher's kid. Most of my young life was spent on the front pew of a church or sleeping underneath that pew! I have loved everything about the church and the Lord's work since I can remember. I went to Bible college at the age of 16. Yes, you read that right: I was sixteen years old when I left home to attend a school that was 3,000 miles away from home. And that is where I fell in love, not with a man, but with the book of Proverbs.

My first personal encounter with the book of Proverbs was in my college dorm room when I came across Proverbs 31. It spoke to me in a profound way and described the kind of woman I aspired to become. I would read it, meditate on it, pray over it, and believe it for my life every day for a little over a month. It seemed that this was the first time that I had allowed the Word to read me as much as I was reading it if that makes sense.

Let's fast forward two years. I married my husband, Ted, who felt God calling him to work in church ministry as well. We started our first full-time church assignment as pastors during our first year of marriage. We also started our family at that time when our first son, Zachary, was born one month after our first wedding anniversary. Two years later, Grant was born and seventeen months later Macie came into the world. From that first assignment, we served as senior pastors for 25 years at four churches in four different states, and this is where my journey gets really interesting.

After 25 years of leading churches, the Lord called us out of full-time church ministry and into the marketplace. No matter how much we were tempted to try and go back into church ministry – because that is what we knew and were comfortable with – we were confident that the Lord was calling us out of our comfort zone. The past years I have felt at times like I was placed in a dark room to be developed as old photos used to be, while at other times it seemed like I was living in a cave as King David had done in his early years. I could also liken that time to a cocoon that has helped me to develop and sprout new wings.

Even though it's been challenging at times, I would not trade this new adventure for the world! I'm grateful for the new ways I have seen God and His people, for the new things He has taught me and continues to teach me – things I thought I understood, but only partially knew. This pivotal point in my life has brought so much freedom and revelation as to who I am in Christ and what He has designed and purposed me to do. I am designed to bring hope to others! This is something that I have always done without even knowing it, which is usually how one's purpose shows up. I just had the misunderstanding that I was to do this strictly within the church walls, but now I see that I was limiting God.

This brings me to why I chose to write this devotional and why it is so important to practice speaking the Word out loud and declaring its truths. When a major shift happens in our lives, we have some choices. We can continue to try with all our might to keep things the same, we can get lost in the shift and lose our way completely, or we can lean in and work through the growth process utilizing and relying on the Word of God to do so.

Declaring the truth of the Word over our lives is a powerful and effective way to utilize God's Word. However, declaration is different than confession or proclamation. According to *Webster's Dictionary*, confession is a disclosure of one's sins or a formal statement of religious beliefs. We confess our sins to God and others as well as confess Jesus as our Lord and Savior. To proclaim means to announce something publicly and/or officially. Proclamation is a public action where confession is a personal one.

A declaration is an announcement, however, a statement made by a party to a legal transaction usually not under oath. When we begin to practice declaring God's Word over our lives, we are utilizing our authority we have been given through Jesus as well as the authority of His Holy Word. We are announcing His truth over our lives. My desire for you as you embark on this 31-day journey is that you will experience the Word of God in a fresh new way and declare it with authority over your life – and then see the results.

Why Proverbs?

Proverbs is a book that teaches us how to deal with the practical things of this world or you could say to exist and thrive in our culture with a Kingdom of God mindset. The book empowers us with wisdom, knowledge, and understanding. We've seen repeatedly that the world traffics in fear, and it is so easy for us to also fall into that trap without even realizing that fear has paralyzed us and stripped us of the blessings God would bestow on us when we obey. It doesn't have to be like this. We have the Kingdom way right at our fingertips and I want you to utilize every tool that is available to live the abundant life God has purposed for you!

It is my desire that this devotional will help you experience and understand the book of Proverbs through a new covenant perspective. It is also my prayer that through this you will read the word of God as it reads you. This isn't just another book to be read as an obligation but rather as a lifeline to the promises of God. The word of God is living and active and vital to our personal relationship with Jesus. I pray that your hunger for intimate relationship with Jesus will be sparked and fanned by this experience and that the word of God will become your daily bread!

When the major shift happened in my life that I mentioned earlier, my Mom was living with us at the time. This wasn't a coincidence but a gift from God. God has a way of orchestrating just what we need when we need it, and God knew I needed my mamma! I needed her voice, her strength, and her wisdom. One particular day, I was so disappointed and disillusioned and I couldn't seem to shake them. Mom always had a special way of gently and lovingly speaking the truth to me. She walked up to me, put her hand on my face, looked me in the eye, and said, "Baby girl, everybody goes through at least one major shift like this in their lifetime and it's better that you're going through it now than later. You'll be stronger and better for it." What a gift! I'm so grateful for a mother who loved Jesus and listened to His voice. She showed me throughout her entire life how to have relationship with the Lord and love Him back. Her love for Proverbs is a big reason I am sharing this with you.

The book of Proverbs has always been a part of my life in one way or another. It all started in the mornings, as early as I can remember. I would walk into the kitchen and see Mom sitting at the table in her robe and slippers, her Bible open and her hands wrapped around a cup of hot coffee. This memory is so vivid because it happened so frequently; I could count on it. This was not a seasonal thing or a fad; it was daily living as natural as eating or bathing. As I got old enough to inquire, I discovered that the book of Proverbs was always on the menu. Sometimes it was the appetizer and sometimes the dessert, but it was always part of Mom's daily bread. Little did Mom know that this simple act of consistency and spiritual formation would impact me forever. (Parents, it matters what our children see when we don't know they are watching!) Once I started on my own personal journey with Proverbs, I realized why Mom would read it every day, month after month, year after year; she was choosing to live by the Word.

My purpose in putting this project together is to help you do the same. I want to help you experience the full, abundant life God designed you to live. God has a divine purpose for your life, something only you can do and be. No one else can accomplish what you are purposed for. His Word helps each of us know Him and ourselves better, embracing our divine design and living our lives by His word.

There are 915 verses in Proverbs, and one in particular inspired me to start making daily declarations: "Death and Life are in the power of the tongue" (Proverbs 18:12). Since death and life are in the power of my words, then what I say matters! I realized that making intentional daily declarations over my life was a key element to my growth and perspective. I need to be reminded on a regular basis that no matter what is happening, God's truth remains and is a firm foundation, a rock. I can count on it. This easy practice of declaring the truth over my life has been a game changer for me and I know it will do the same for you.

What You Can Expect

So here is how this book is designed to work. Proverbs is full of truth, wisdom, and insight for living and is perfect to read each day. There are thirty-one chapters, one for each day of the month. What I have written for each day begins with a devotional thought and the passage from Proverbs for that day, as well as some daily declarations. You will then have the opportunity to write down the personal revelation you received while reading and meditating on that daily passage. You can also then record how you will apply the truth of the revelation you received and I have provided space for you to write your own personal declaration to supplement mine. I strongly encourage you to prayerfully read the chapter for the day and the declarations, then speak the declarations out loud over your life. You may want to read it out loud a few times until you are able to confidently declare it over your situation and in your life.

I am thrilled that you are joining me on this journey as part of your spiritual formation and I pray that your life will be forever transformed as you read, pray, and declare the truth over your life, your family and your friends.

Tami Miller
Arlington, Texas
October 2023

PROVERBS 1

Within the first month of our major shift to market-place ministry, I received a prophetic word. The Bible tells us in 1 Thessalonians 5:19-21, "Do not quench the Spirit. Do not treat prophecies with contempt but test them all; hold on to what is good." Part of this prophecy was describing a physical home the Lord was preparing for us with a unique fireplace and surroundings that looked like a Thomas Kinkade painting. I liked the sound of that so I kept it in my heart and held on to it.

Two years and two states later and during the pandemic, we purchased a home online without seeing it in person. When we came to look at the property (48 hour before our earnest money was non-refundable), I was amazed by what the Lord had prepared for us. He knew exactly what we needed, and He kept His word. I have a beautiful, unique fireplace and our neighborhood is literally called, "Forest Hills." We can't ever give up on the promises of God! His word is yes and amen. We might not see the fruition of His promises immediately or when we think we need them but He will come through. We are God's kids and He loves taking care of us.

****

Proverbs 1:1-10 – Here are kingdom revelations, words to live by, and words of wisdom given to empower you to reign in life, written as proverbs by Israel's King Solomon, David's son. Within these sayings will be found the revelation of wisdom and the impartation of spiritual understanding. Use them as keys to unlock the treasures of true knowledge. Those who cling to these words will receive discipline to demonstrate wisdom in every relationship and to choose what is right and just and fair. These proverbs will give you great skill to teach the immature and make them wise, to give youth the understanding of their design and destiny.

For the wise, these proverbs will make you even wiser, and for those with discernment, you will be able to acquire brilliant strategies for leadership. These kingdom revelations will break open your understanding to unveil the deeper meaning of parables, poetic riddles, and epigrams, and to unravel the words and enigmas of the wise. We cross the threshold of true knowledge when we live in obedient devotion to God. Stubborn know-it-alls will never stop to do this, for they scorn true wisdom and knowledge. Pay close attention, my child, to your father's wise words and never forget your mother's instructions. For their insight will bring you success, adorning you with grace-filled thoughts and giving you reins to guide your decisions. When peer pressure compels you to go with the crowd and sinners invite you to join in, you must simply say, "No!"

****

Proverbs 1:20-21 – Wisdom's praises are sung in the streets and celebrated far and wide. Yet wisdom's song is not always heard in the halls of higher learning. But in the hustle and bustle of everyday life its lyrics can always be heard above the din of the crowd. You will hear wisdom's warning as she preaches courageously to those who stop to listen.

****

Proverbs 1:33 – But the one who always listens to me will live undisturbed in a heavenly peace. Free from fear, confident and courageous, that one will rest unafraid and sheltered from the storms of life."

Declarations

- These proverbs teach me wisdom and discipline, helping me to intentionally live out my God given purpose.
- I have a teachable spirit and respond to correction with humility and openness.
- I choose the fear of the Lord: living in respect, acknowledgement, and awe of Him.
- I am continually growing in awareness of His involvement in my life.
- I live in awe and wonder that He is with me.
- I love wisdom and instruction and tune my ear to it.
- I am safe. I am secure. Safety and security are my promises from God and He keeps His promises. I am His.

My Personal Revelation of Wisdom

_____

_____

_____

_____

_____

_____

My Personal Applications

_____

_____

_____

_____

_____

My Personal Declarations

_____

_____

_____

_____

_____

"God's wisdom will become visible by those who embrace it" (Matthew 11:19b).

PROVERBS 2

Have you ever misunderstood, or perhaps not understood at all, what God was doing in your life? There have been many times in my life when I could not see the forest from the trees. All I could see was right in front of me – and it didn't look good. I began to realize that this was when I need to trust God more, not less. At the time of my transition out of church work, I felt as if everything that I knew was being ripped away.

One day, I was recounting to God all the things I had lost, having a pity party with me as the guest of honor. It was then that I heard the Holy Spirit clearly say to me, "What you think is your loss is for your deliverance." With those words, I was undone! I came to the realization that God was delivering me and keeping me in the way of His goodness and on the path He had planned, and that changed my perspective of what I was walking through. He could see the beginning from the end – the whole picture not just my perspective of it. I began to release what I was trying to control so I could learn to trust God at a deeper level. God knows what is best for you. Learn to lean on Him and trust Him more!

****

Proverbs 2:1-12 – My child, will you treasure my wisdom? Then, and only then, will you acquire it. And only if you accept my advice and hide it within will you succeed. So train your heart to listen when I speak and open your spirit wide to expand your discernment—then pass it on to your sons and daughters. Yes, cry out for comprehension and intercede for insight. For if you keep seeking it like a man would seek for sterling silver, searching in hidden places for cherished treasure, then you will discover the fear of the Lord and find the true knowledge of God. Wisdom is a gift from a generous God, and every word he speaks is full of revelation and becomes a fountain of understanding within you.

For the Lord has a hidden storehouse of wisdom made

accessible to his godly ones. He becomes your personal bodyguard as you follow his ways, protecting and guarding you as you choose what is right. Then you will discover all that is just, proper, and fair, and be empowered to make the right decisions as you walk into your destiny. When wisdom wins your heart and revelation breaks in, true pleasure enters your soul. If you choose to follow good counsel, divine design will watch over you and understanding will protect you from making poor choices. It will rescue you from evil in disguise and from those who speak duplicities.

****

Proverbs 2:20-21 – Follow those who follow wisdom and stay on the right path. For all my godly lovers will enjoy life to the fullest and will inherit their destinies.

Declarations

- Proverbs teaches me wisdom and discipline, helping me to intentionally live out my God-given purpose.
- I have a teachable spirit and respond to correction with humility and openness.
- I choose the fear of the Lord: living in respect, acknowledgment, and awe of Him.
- I am aware of His involvement in my life.
- I live in awe and wonder that He is with me.
- I love wisdom and instruction and tune my ear to it.
- Safety and security are my promises from God and He keeps His promises. I am safe. I am secure. I am His.

My Personal Revelation of Wisdom

_____

_____

_____

_____

_____

_____

My Personal Applications

_____

_____

_____

_____

_____

My Personal Declarations

_____

_____

_____

_____

_____

"We have become his poetry, a re-created people that will fulfill the destiny he has given each of us, for we are joined to Jesus, the Anointed One. Even before we were born, God planned in advance our destiny and the good works we would do to fulfill it!" (Ephesians 2:10).

PROVERBS 3

Our Proverb for today talks about trusting God and the promises you receive as you live by His word along with an increased awareness of His involvement in your everyday life. Before you read it, I want you to look at a familiar story in Mathew 14:22-32 when Peter asked the question, "Lord, is it you?" This question signifies a desire to see Jesus more clearly in the middle of our situation and is one I'm learning to ask on a more regular basis.

The disciples sailed out into the middle of the lake and a huge storm came up. The Bible says they were very afraid when they saw someone walking on the water in the middle of the storm, thinking it was a ghost. Jesus identified himself and Peter said, "Lord if it's you, ask me to come out on the water with you!" That is just what Jesus did. You probably know the rest of the story. Peter walked on water toward Jesus until he put his eyes on his circumstance and took them off Jesus. As Peter began to sink, he cried out to the Lord to save him. Jesus immediately reached out His hand and lifted him up saying, "What little faith you have. Why would you let doubt win?" Jesus and Peter both walked back to the boat and immediately the storm stopped!

What if we would ask in the middle of our life storms, "Lord, is it you?" I firmly believe that in every life situation God wants us to reveal Himself to us in a new way so we can learn more about Him and His goodness. He is big enough to meet us right where we are and walk with us through the hardest of times.

For example, when I was losing my dad to cancer, I experienced God as my comforter, strength, and a good Father. God didn't cause my dad to die, but He met me there and was with me through it. I just had to look into my storm for His movement and ask, "Lord is that you?" Are you looking for Him while you're in the middle of a storm? It takes faith to get your eyes off your circumstance long enough to see what God might be showing you about Himself that you haven't yet experienced. It is so easy to only see what is happening to us in the moment, like the disciples did in the storm and stay focused on that instead of putting our eyes on the Lord – no matter what is happening around you.

If you are going through sickness look to your Healer. If you are going through financial strain, look to your Provider. God wants you to walk with Him and learn to trust Him while we asking and get the answers to, "Lord, is it You?"

****

Proverbs 3:1-26 – My child, if you truly want a long and satisfying life, never forget the things that I've taught you. Follow closely every truth that I've given you. Then you will have a full, rewarding life. Hold on to loyal love and don't let go, and be faithful to all that you've been taught. Let your life be shaped by integrity, with truth written upon your heart. That's how you will find favor and understanding with both God and men—you will gain the reputation of living life well.

Trust in the Lord completely, and do not rely on your own opinions. With all your heart rely on him to guide you, and he will lead you in every decision you make. Become intimate with him in whatever you do, and he will lead you wherever you go. Don't think for a moment that you know it all, for wisdom comes when you adore him with undivided devotion and avoid everything that's wrong. Then you will find the healing refreshment your body and spirit long for. Glorify God with all your wealth, honoring him with your firstfruits, with every increase that comes to you. Then every dimension of your life will overflow with blessings from an uncontainable source of inner joy!

My child, when the Lord God speaks to you, never take his words lightly, and never be upset when he corrects you. For the Father's discipline comes only from his passionate love and pleasure for you. Even when it seems like his correction is harsh, it's still better than any father on earth gives to his child. Blessings pour over the ones who find wisdom, for they have obtained living-understanding. As wisdom increases, a great treasure is imparted, greater than many bars of refined gold. It is a more valuable commodity than gold and gemstones, for there is nothing you desire that could compare to her. Wisdom extends to you long life in one hand and wealth and promotion in the other. Out of her mouth flows righteousness, and her words release both law and mercy.

The ways of wisdom are sweet, always drawing you into the place of wholeness. Seeking for her brings the discovery of untold blessings, for she is the healing tree of life to those who taste her fruits. The Lord laid the earth's foundations with wisdom's blueprints. By his living-understanding all the universe came into being. By his divine revelation he broke open the hidden fountains of the deep, bringing secret springs to the surface as the mist of the night dripped down from heaven.

My child, never drift off course from these two goals for your life: to walk in wisdom and to discover your purpose. Don't ever forget how they empower you. For they strengthen you inside and out and inspire you to do what's right; you will be energized and refreshed by the healing they bring. They give you living hope to guide you, and not one of life's tests will cause you to stumble. You will sleep like a baby, safe and sound—your rest will be sweet and secure. You will not be subject to terror, for it will not terrify you. Nor will the disrespectful be able to push you aside, because God is your confidence in times of crisis, keeping your heart at rest in every situation.

Declarations

- I live in the fear of the Lord.
- I remember His word and act on it.
- I am productive and peaceful and have a long life ahead of me.
- Mercy and truth are with me from the inside out.
- I have favor with God and others.
- I trust in the Lord with my whole being.
- I lean on Him and not on myself.
- I acknowledge the Lord and live in increased awareness of Him.
- I am confident to ask, "Lord, is this You?"

My Personal Revelation of Wisdom

_____

_____

_____

_____

_____

_____

My Personal Applications

_____

_____

_____

_____

_____

_____

My Personal Declarations

_____

_____

_____

_____

_____

"For it is not from man that we draw our life but from God as we are being joined to Jesus, the Anointed One. And now he is our God-given wisdom, our virtue, our holiness, and our redemption"
(1 Corinthians 1:30).

PROVERBS 4

How do you guard the affections of your heart? I believe that it starts with your thoughts. How and what you are thinking proceeds from how you feel and what you do. Let's go a step further, for your thoughts also influence what you say. Matthew 12:34b states, "Out of the abundance of the heart the mouth speaks." No wonder you are considered wise when you guard the affections of your heart.

I first began to learn to guard the affections of my heart was just a few weeks after September 11, 2001. We had just relocated from Northwest Arkansas to Southern California and as you can imagine, our cost of living was significantly higher and we had moved in faith taking a 20% decrease in pay. My fear and negativity were at their peak. My toxic thought life was affecting me emotionally, physically, and spiritually. I finally reached my breaking point and decided that I had to do something different.

I couldn't change that our nation had been attacked or that we lived in a new season with very little to live on and three children under the age of seven to provide for. But I realized I could change how I was thinking. I got out my Bible and 3-by-5 index cards and began to write out the truth and promises of God. I placed my cards all over the house, on my bathroom mirror, kitchen sink, refrigerator. You get the picture – they were everywhere! Each time I saw them, I would read them out loud. I did this over and over again. I began to think better and feel better and talk better. This simple practice changed my life and taught me the power of activating God's word in my life as a guard over the affections of my heart!

****

Proverbs 4:1-14 – Listen to my correction, my sons, for I speak to you as your father. Let discernment enter your heart and you will grow wise with the understanding I impart. My revelation-truth is a gift to you, so remain faithful to my instruction. For I, too, was once the delight of my father and cherished by my mother—their beloved child. Then my father taught me, saying, "Never forget my words. If you do everything that I teach you, you will reign in life." So make wisdom your quest—search for the revelation of life's meaning. Don't let what I say go in one ear and out the other.

Stick with wisdom and she will stick to you, protecting you throughout your days. She will rescue all those who passionately listen to her voice. Wisdom is the most valuable commodity—so buy it! Revelation-knowledge is what you need—so invest in it! Wisdom will exalt you when you exalt her truth. She will lead you to honor and favor when you live your life by her insights. You will be adorned with beauty and grace, and wisdom's glory will wrap itself around you, making you victorious in the race. My son, if you will take the time to stop and listen to me and embrace what I say, you will live a long and happy life full of understanding in every way.

I have taken you by the hand in wisdom's ways, pointing you to the path of integrity. Your progress will have no limits when you come along with me, and you will never stumble as you walk along the way. So receive my correction no matter how hard it is to swallow, for wisdom will snap you back into place—her words will be invigorating life to you. Do not detour into darkness or even set foot on that path.

****

Proverbs 4:20-27 – Listen carefully, my dear child, to everything that I teach you, and pay attention to all that I have to say. Fill your thoughts with my words until they penetrate deep into your spirit. Then, as you unwrap my words, they will impart true life and radiant health into the very core of your being. So above all, guard the affections of your heart, for they affect all that you are.

Pay attention to the welfare of your innermost being, for from there flows the wellspring of life. Avoid dishonest speech and pretentious words. Be free from using perverse words no matter what! Set your gaze on the path before you. With fixed purpose, looking straight ahead, *ignore life's distractions.* Watch where you're going! Stick to the path of truth, and the road will be safe and smooth before you. Don't allow yourself to be sidetracked for even a moment or take the detour that leads to darkness.

Declarations

- I value the wisdom of God and remain faithful to it.
- As I receive God's wisdom and instruction, I share it with others.
- I fill my thoughts with the words and wisdom of God.
- These words bring me true life and health.
- I guard the affections of my heart and care for my inmost being.
- My self-care starts with my spirit and keeps me on the path of truth.

My Personal Revelation of Wisdom

_____

_____

_____

_____

_____

_____

My Personal Applications

_____

_____

_____

_____

_____

_____

My Personal Declarations

_____

_____

_____

_____

_____

"Your Word is a lamp to guide my feet
and a light for my path"
(Psalms 119:105, NLT).

PROVERBS 5

When I was growing up, Mom always said, "You have to get to the root of the problem." If you're not careful you will spend a lot of your life dealing with the reaction to the root problem and not the real issue. Your focus will be on your behavior and not the heart of the matter. To help us to get to the "root" you must learn how to apply and then activate the wisdom of God in your life.

Picture with me a water filter, most of us have one either in our refrigerator or use a free-standing pitcher type. We use these to help get the impurities out of our drinking water and ultimately to help our water taste better. Now think about the wisdom of God in this context. If we pour everything in our lives through the filter of God's wisdom, we begin to taste, see, and do things differently. Our involvement with and awareness of Him and His ways increase which gets us to the "root" of what we are dealing with. This also protects us from the impurities that would otherwise pollute or even destroy us.

When you acknowledge God in your everyday life and look to involve Him and apply His wisdom, you are correcting the root problem, which is your tendency to go astray like the sheep that we all are. Activating that wisdom will become your spiritual GPS that will get you right where you need to be in God every time.

****

Proverbs 5:1-2 – Listen to me, my son, for I know what I'm talking about. Listen carefully to my advice so that wisdom and discernment will enter your heart, and then the words you speak will express what you've learned.

****

Proverbs 5:21-23 – For God sees everything you do and his eyes are wide open as he observes every single habit you have. Beware that your sins don't overtake you and that the scars of your own conscience don't become the ropes that tie you up. Those who choose wickedness die for lack of self-control, for their foolish ways lead them astray, carrying them away as hostages—*kidnapped captives robbed of destiny.*

Declarations

- I am a child of God.
- I live in an increased awareness of Holy Spirit working in my life.
- I have the protection and benefits that discretion, discernment and wisdom offer me.
- I listen carefully to God's word and obey Him.
- I am a doer of the word and not a hearer only.
- I live to please Him.

My Personal Revelation of Wisdom

_____

_____

_____

_____

_____

_____

My Personal Applications

_____

_____

_____

_____

_____

_____

My Personal Declarations

_____

_____

_____

_____

_____

"Keep creating in me a clean heart. Fill me with pure thoughts and holy desires, ready to please you" (Psalm 51:10).

PROVERBS 6

We have a saying in the Miller home, "Everything is a seed!" The principle behind our saying is that seeds are powerful and produce after their own kind. If we plant an apple seed, we will get an apple tree. If we plant corn, we get corn. One seed has the potential to produce a bountiful harvest.

Galatians 6:7 says, "Do not be deceived, God is not mocked; whatsoever a man sows, that he will also reap." So the question is then what type of seed are you planting? Are you planting faithfulness and love? Loyalty and trust? Are you planting kindness and joy or are you planting selfishness and hatred?

Living your life acknowledging that everything you do and say is a seed can be sobering and freeing. It is sobering because you all have seeds you wish you hadn't planted. You are hoping for a crop failure, but wouldn't you know it, you find an abundant harvest. The good news is that you can start planting new seed today and can then expect a new and better harvest in due time.

Everything is a seed! That being said, what will you plant today?

****

Proverbs 6:6-23 – When you're feeling lazy, come and learn a lesson from this tale of the tiny ant. Yes, all you lazybones, come learn from the example of the ant and enter into wisdom. The ants have no chief, no boss, no manager—no one has to tell them what to do. You'll see them working and toiling all summer long, stockpiling their food in preparation for winter. So wake up, sleepyhead. How long will you lie there? When will you wake up and get out of bed? If you keep nodding off and thinking, "I'll do it later," or say to yourself, "I'll just sit back awhile and take it easy," just watch how the future unfolds! By making excuses you'll learn what it means to go without. Poverty will pounce on you like a bandit and move in as your roommate for life.

Here's another life lesson to learn from observing wayward and wicked men. You can tell they are lawless. They're constant liars, proud deceivers, full of clever ploys and convincing plots. Their twisted thoughts are perverse, and they are always scheming to stir up trouble, and sowing strife with every step they take. But when calamity comes knocking on their door, suddenly and without warning they're undone—broken to bits, shattered, with no hope of healing.

There are six evils God truly hates and a seventh that is an abomination to him: Putting others down while considering yourself superior, spreading lies and rumors, spilling the blood of the innocent, plotting evil in your heart toward another, gloating over doing what's plainly wrong, spouting lies in false testimony, and stirring up strife *between friends*. These are entirely despicable to God!

My son, obey your father's godly instruction and follow your mother's life-giving teaching. Fill your heart with their advice and let your life be shaped by what they've taught you. Their wisdom will guide you wherever you go and keep you from bringing harm to yourself. Their instruction will whisper to you at every sunrise and direct you through a brand-new day. For truth is a bright beam of light shining into every area of your life, instructing and correcting you to discover the ways to godly living.

Declarations

- I plant good seed that yields a good crop of righteousness.
- God's truth protects me at all times, while teaching me His ways.
- I am humble.
- I build others up. I am loyal, faithful, and can be trusted.
- I am a peacemaker.
- I am a hard worker.
- All that I do, I do for the Lord.
- I am thankful for God and His word that speaks to me, leads me, and keeps me.
- I live by His Word.

My Personal Revelation of Wisdom

_____

_____

_____

_____

_____

_____

My Personal Applications

_____

_____

_____

_____

_____

My Personal Declarations

_____

_____

_____

_____

_____

"Put your heart and soul into every activity you do, as though you are doing it for the Lord himself and not merely for others" (Colossians 3:23).

PROVERBS 7

Did you know that the phrase "the apple of my eye" is used on four occasions in the Bible in Deuteronomy, Psalms, Proverbs, and Lamentations? We sometimes use this phrase to describe someone we cherish. In Hebrew, this statement is actually translated as "little man of his eye" when that causes me to think of how we can sometimes see a reflection of ourselves in the pupil of someone else's eye. I am looking at them, but I see me. That's how it is with God's word it is a mirror that shows us who we are and where we're actually at in our walk with Him:

> For the word of God is alive and active. Sharper than any double-edged sword, it penetrates even to dividing soul and spirit, joints and marrow; it judges the thoughts and attitudes of the heart. [13] Nothing in all creation is hidden from God's sight. Everything is uncovered and laid bare before the eyes of him to whom we must give account (Hebrews 4:11-12, NIV).

In our declarations today, we are proclaiming, "God's words and His ways are the apple of my eye." This means we are cherishing His words and our identity is found as we reflect Him through His Word.

*****

> Proverbs 7:1-5 – Stick close to my instruction, my son, and follow all my advice. If you do what I say you will live well. Guard your life with my revelation-truth, for my teaching is as precious as your eyesight. Treasure my instructions, and cherish them within your heart. Say to wisdom, "I love you," and to understanding, "You're my sweetheart." "May the two of you protect me, and may we never be apart!" For they will keep you from the adulteress, with her smooth words meant to seduce your heart.

Declarations

- God's Word and His ways are the apple of my eye.
- I cherish His Word.
- God's Word protects me from self-deception as I apply His directives to my life.
- I have full and abundant life.
- I keep His Word in my heart.
- I declare His Word with my mouth.
- I live by His Word!

My Personal Revelation of Wisdom

_____

_____

_____

_____

_____

_____

My Personal Applications

_____

_____

_____

_____

_____

My Personal Declarations

_____

_____

_____

_____

_____

"Don't just listen to the Word of Truth and not respond to it, for that is the essence of self-deception. So always let his Word become like poetry written and fulfilled by your life!" (James 1:22).

PROVERBS 8

When my kids were going into high school I told them, "You'll find what you're looking for." I wanted them to learn that what they would seek, they would find. If they were looking for friends, they would find friends. If they were looking for answers, they would come. If they were looking for trouble, that would come too.

The same is true for you today. The problem then and now is that when you don't seek what you need or want, things find you that you don't need or want. Mathew 6:33 says, "But seek first the kingdom of God and His righteousness, and all these things shall be added to you." Let's not be passive in our relationship with Jesus. Rather, let's seek Him and His Kingdom!

****

Proverbs 8:1-21 – Can't you hear the voice of Wisdom? From the top of the mountains of influence she speaks into the gateways of the glorious city. At the place where pathways merge, at the entrance of every portal, there she stands, ready to impart understanding, shouting aloud to all who enter, preaching her sermon to those who will listen.

"I'm calling to you, sons of Adam, yes, and to you daughters as well. Listen to me and you will be prudent and wise. For even the foolish and feeble can receive an understanding heart *that will change their inner being.* The meaning of my words will release within you revelation for you to reign in life. My lyrics will empower you to live by what is right. For everything I say is unquestionably true, and I refuse to endure the lies of lawlessness—my words will never lead you astray.

"All the declarations of my mouth can be trusted; they contain no twisted logic or perversion of the truth. All my words are clear and straightforward to everyone who possesses spiritual understanding. If you have an open mind, you will receive revelation-knowledge. My wise correction is more valuable than silver or gold. The finest gold is nothing compared to the revelation-knowledge I can impart."

Wisdom is so priceless that it exceeds the value of any jewel. Nothing you could wish for can equal her. "For I am Wisdom, and I am shrewd and intelligent. I have at my disposal living-understanding to devise a plan for your life. Wisdom pours into you when you begin to hate every form of evil in your life, for that's what worship and fearing God is all about. Then you will discover that your pompous pride and perverse speech are the very ways of wickedness that I hate!"

"You will find true success when you find me, for I have insight into wise plans that are designed just for you. I hold in my hands living-understanding, courage, and strength. I empower kings to reign and rulers to make laws that are just. I empower princes to rise and take dominion, and generous ones to govern the earth. I will show my love to those who passionately love me. For they will search and search continually until they find me. Unending wealth and glory come to those who discover where I dwell. The riches of righteousness and a long, satisfying life will be given to them. What I impart has greater worth than gold and treasure, and the increase I bring benefits more than a windfall of income. I lead you into the ways of righteousness to discover the paths of true justice. Those who love me gain great wealth and a glorious inheritance, and I will fill their lives with treasures."

****

Proverbs 8:32-35 – "So listen, my sons and daughters, to everything I tell you, for nothing will bring you more joy than following my ways. Listen to my counsel, for my instruction will enlighten you. You'll be wise not to ignore it. If you wait at wisdom's doorway, longing to hear a word for every day, joy will break forth within you as you listen for what I'll say. For the fountain of life pours into you every time that you find me, and this is the secret of growing in the delight and the favor of the Lord.

Declarations

- I seek the wisdom of God and depend on it for a successful life.
- God's ways are higher than mine and wisdom is His right-hand-man. I receive and apply wisdom's instruction.
- I walk in humility and honor God in my life.
- I keep God's ways and acknowledge Him in everything that I do.
- In finding wisdom, I am blessed.
- I have abundant life and favor from God!

My Personal Revelation of Wisdom

_____

_____

_____

_____

_____

My Personal Applications

_____

_____

_____

_____

_____

My Personal Declarations

_____

_____

_____

_____

_____

"In the beginning was the Word, and the
Word was with God, and the Word was
God. He was in the beginning with God.
All things were made through Him, and
without Him nothing was made that was
made" (John 1:1-3, NKJV).

PROVERBS 9

In the book of Proverbs, we see that the fear of the Lord is discussed quite a bit. To have a healthy fear of God doesn't mean that we are afraid of him in the sense that he is an out-to-get-us angry God. To fear Him literally means to have a moral reverence for Him, to be in awe of Him and to respect Him. I liken it to acknowledging Him and His ways in my everyday life and yielding to the nudging of Holy Spirit. Living in the wisdom way is living in the fear of God.

****

Proverbs 9:1-12 – Wisdom has built herself a palace upon seven pillars to keep it secure. She has made ready a banquet feast and the sacrifice has been killed. She has mingled her wine, and the table's all set. She has sent out her maidens, crying out from the high place, inviting everyone to come and eat until they're full.

"Whoever wants to know me and receive my wisdom, come and dine at my table and drink of my wine. Lay aside your simple thoughts and leave your paths behind. Agree with my ways, live in my truth, and you will find righteousness."

If you try to correct an arrogant cynic, expect an angry insult in return. And if you try to confront an evil man, don't be surprised if all you get is a slap in the face! So don't even bother to correct a mocker, for he'll only hate you for it. But go ahead and correct the wise; they'll love you even more.

Teach a wise man what is right and he'll grow even wiser. Instruct the lovers of God and they'll learn even more. The starting point for acquiring wisdom is to be consumed with awe as you worship Yahweh. To receive the revelation of the Holy One, you must come to the one who has living-understanding. Wisdom will extend your life, making every year more fruitful than the one before.

So it is to your advantage to be wise. But to ignore the counsel of wisdom is to invite trouble into your life.

Declarations

- I seek wisdom.
- I listen to and for wisdom.
- I walk with the wise and assimilate their wisdom.
- I have good judgment and it originates in the knowledge of God.
- I acknowledge Him in everything I do and everywhere that I go.
- I choose the Wisdom Way.

My Personal Revelation of Wisdom

_____

_____

_____

_____

_____

My Personal Applications

_____

_____

_____

_____

_____

My Personal Declarations

_____

_____

_____

_____

_____

"For of Him and through Him and to Him
are all things, to whom be glory forever.
Amen" (Romans 11:36, NKJV).

PROVERBS 10

Our love for God is in response to Him loving us first. Because of His great love for us, He gave His only son as a sacrifice for us all! Jesus is perfect wisdom and in Him we live and move and have our being! It amazes me to think about all that Jesus has done for us through his life, death and resurrection and to top it off, He sent Holy Spirit to seal the deal! Now we get to re-gift Him with our lives. This is how we love Him back!

****

Proverbs 10:3-12 – The Lord satisfies the longings of all his lovers, but he withholds from the wicked what their souls crave. Slackers will know what it means to be poor, while the hard worker becomes wealthy. Know the importance of the season you're in and a wise son you will be. But what a waste when an incompetent son sleeps through his day of opportunity!

The lover of God is enriched beyond belief, but the evil man only curses his luck. The reputation of the righteous becomes a sweet memorial to him, while the wicked life only leaves a rotten stench. The heart of the wise will easily accept instruction. But those who do all the talking are too busy to listen and learn. They'll just keep stumbling ahead into the mess they created. The one who walks in integrity will experience a fearless confidence in life, but the one who is devious will eventually be exposed.

The troublemaker always has a clever plan and won't look you in the eye, but the one who speaks correction honestly can be trusted to make peace. The teachings of the lovers of God are like living truth flowing from the fountain of life, but the words of the wicked hide an ulterior motive. Hatred keeps old quarrels alive, but love draws a veil over every insult and finds a way to make sin disappear.

****

Proverbs 10:16 – The lovers of God earn their wages for

a life of righteousness, but the wages of the wicked are squandered on a life of sin.

****

Proverbs 10:19-22 – If you keep talking, it won't be long before you're saying something really wrong. Prove you're wise from the very start—just bite your tongue and be strong! The teachings of the godly ones are like pure silver, bringing words of redemption to others, but the heart of the wicked is corrupt. The lovers of God feed many with their teachings, but the foolish ones starve themselves for lack of an understanding heart. True enrichment comes from the blessing of the Lord, with rest and contentment in knowing that it all comes from him.

****

Proverbs 10:25 – The wicked are blown away by every stormy wind. But when a catastrophe comes, the lovers of God have a secure anchor.

****

Proverbs 10:27-32 – Living in the worship and awe of God will bring you many years of contented living. So how could the wicked ever expect to have a long, happy life? Lovers of God have a joyful feast of gladness, but the ungodly see their hopes vanish right before their eyes. The beautiful ways of God are a safe resting place for those who have integrity. But to those who work wickedness the ways of God spell doom. God's lover can never be greatly shaken. But the wicked will never inherit the covenant blessings. The teachings of the righteous are loaded with wisdom, but the words of the evil ones are crooked and perverse. Words that bring delight pour from the lips of the godly, but the words of the wicked are duplicitous.

Declarations

- I am a lover of God.
- He loved me first and I get to love Him back.
- I show His love to the world around me.
- God is my anchor in every storm.
- God's ways are my firm footing where I find rest and strength.
- Through my words and actions, I re-gift Him, bringing life and peace to others.
- I am blessed to be a blessing in all I say and all I do.

My Personal Revelation of Wisdom

_____

_____

_____

_____

_____

_____

My Personal Applications

_____

_____

_____

_____

_____

My Personal Declarations

_____

_____

_____

_____

_____

"This is how we have discovered love's
reality: Jesus sacrificed his life for us.
Because of this great love, we should
be willing to lay down our lives for one
another" (1 John 3:16).

PROVERBS 11

There are times when my circumstances seem to be bigger than I am and more than I can handle. When that happens, I become discouraged and overwhelmed. Recently, I reflected on the truth found in Colossians 1:27, " … Christ in you the hope of glory," specifically focusing on the phrase "Christ in me." Colossians 3:3 says, "For you died, and your life is hidden with Christ in God." Then that gave me pause to think about "me in Jesus." Christ in me and I am in Christ.

If I am in Jesus, then that means He must be in my circumstances with me. If He is in me, it also must mean that I am in my circumstances along with Him. Either way, I am a partner and a companion with Christ. Let that sink in. Think about what you are going through right now and picture yourself *in Him* and *Him in you*.

****

Proverbs 11:1-11 – Dishonest business practice is something that Yahweh truly hates. But it pleases him when we apply the right standards of measurement. When you act with presumption, convinced that you're right, don't be surprised if you fall flat on your face! But humility leads to wisdom. Integrity will lead you to success, but treachery will destroy your dreams.

When judgment day comes, all the wealth of the world won't help you one bit. So be rich in righteousness, for that's the only thing that can save you in death. Those with good character walk on a smooth path, with no detour or deviation. But the wicked keep falling because of their own wickedness. Integrity will keep a good man from falling. But the unbeliever is trapped, held captive to his sinful desires. When an evil man dies, all hope is lost, for his misplaced confidence goes in the coffin, buried along with him.

The righteous are snatched away from trouble, and the

wicked show up in their place. The teachings of hypo-crites can destroy you, but revelation-knowledge will res-cue the righteous. The blessing that rests on the righteous releases strength and favor to the entire city, but shouts of joy will be heard when the wicked one dies. The blessing of favor resting upon the righteous influences a city to lift it higher, but wicked leaders tear it apart by their words.

****

Proverbs 11:17-19 – A man of kindness attracts favor, while a cruel man attracts nothing but trouble. Evil peo-ple may get a short-term gain, but to sow seeds of righ-teousness will bring a true and lasting reward. A son of righteousness experiences the abundant life, but the one who pursues evil hurries to his own death.

****

Proverbs 11:23-31 – True lovers of God are filled with longings for what is pleasing and good, but the wicked can only expect doom. Generosity brings prosperity, but withholding from charity brings poverty. Those who live to bless others will have blessings heaped upon them, and the one who pours out his life to pour out blessings will be saturated with favor. People will curse the business-man with no ethics, but the one with a social conscience receives praise from all.

Living your life seeking what is good for others brings untold favor, but those who wish evil for others will find it coming back on them. Keep trusting in your riches and down you'll go! But the lovers of God rise up like flow-ers in the spring. The fool who brings trouble to his own family will be cut out of the will, and the family servant will do better than he. But a life lived loving God bears lasting fruit, for the one who is truly wise wins souls. If the righteous are barely saved, what's in store for all the wicked?

Declarations

- I am the righteousness of God in Christ Jesus.
- Humility and generosity are my way of life.
- Integrity and right standing with God lead to my deliverance.
- Giving mercy and kindness to those around me does good for my own soul.
- I am in Christ Jesus and He is in me!

My Personal Revelation of Wisdom

_____

_____

_____

_____

_____

My Personal Applications

_____

_____

_____

_____

_____

My Personal Declarations

_____

_____

_____

_____

_____

"I am my lover's, and my lover is mine. ...
My lover is mine, and I am his"
(Song of Songs 2:3a, 16a, NLT).

PROVERBS 12

Re-presenting Jesus is living for God loudly and clearly, not just with our words but with our actions. There is a story in Mark 8:23-26 where Jesus healed a blind man. He then told him to go back to his village but not to tell anyone that he had been healed. I'm sure that his entire village knew that he had been blind so when he appeared and could see, his words were louder than his actions. In essence, Jesus had told this man, "Don't use your words of what I have done for you, show them that you can see." What if we became more intentional like that to show people the effects of our relationship with Jesus so our actions would speak louder than our words?

****

Proverbs 12:1-3 – To learn the truth you must long to be teachable, or you can despise correction and remain ignorant. If your heart is right, favor flows from the Lord, but a devious heart invites his condemnation. You can't expect success by doing what's wrong. But the lives of his lovers are deeply rooted and firmly planted.

****

Proverbs 12:6-14 – The wicked use their words to ambush and accuse, but the lovers of God speak to defend and protect. The wicked are taken out, gone for good, but the godly families shall live on. Everyone admires a man of principles, but the one with a corrupt heart is despised. Just be who you are and work hard for a living, for that's better than pretending to be important and starving to death. A good man takes care of the needs of his pets, while even the kindest acts of a wicked man are still cruel. Work hard at your job and you'll have what you need. Following a get-rich-quick scheme is nothing but a fantasy. The cravings of the wicked are only for what is evil, but righteousness is the core motivation for the lovers of God, and it keeps them content and flourishing. The wicked will get trapped by their words of gossip, slander, and lies. But for the righteous, honesty is its own defense. For there is great satisfaction in speaking the truth, and hard work brings blessings back to you.

****

Proverbs 12:18-28 – Reckless words are like the thrusts of a sword, cutting remarks meant to stab and to hurt. But the words of the wise soothe and heal. Truthful words will stand the test of time, but one day every lie will be seen for what it is. Deception fills the hearts of those who plot harm, but those who plan for peace are filled with joy. Calamity is not allowed to overwhelm the righteous, but there's nothing but trouble waiting for the wicked. Live in the truth and keep your promises, and the Lord will keep delighting in you, but he detests a liar.

Those who possess wisdom don't feel the need to impress others with what they know, but foolish ones make sure their ignorance is on display. If you want to reign in life, don't sit on your hands. Instead, work hard at doing what's right, for the slacker will end up working to make someone else succeed. Anxious fear brings depression, but a life-giving word of encouragement can do wonders to restore joy to the heart. Lovers of God give good advice to their friends, but the counsel of the wicked will lead them astray. A passive person won't even complete a project, but a passionate person makes good use of his time, wealth, and energy. Abundant life is discovered by walking in righteousness, but holding on to your anger leads to death.

Declarations

- I am the righteousness of God in Christ Jesus.
- In Him I have life.
- In Him I have favor.
- I have a teachable spirit.
- In Him my mind is renewed.
- My words promote health to all who hear – and to me.
- I work hard and produce good fruit because I am in Him.
- In Him I come through trouble and bring on peace.
- He delights in me, and He knows me. I know Him and delight in Him!
- I am in Christ and Christ is in me.

My Personal Revelation of Wisdom

_____

_____

_____

_____

_____

My Personal Applications

_____

_____

_____

_____

_____

_____

My Personal Declarations

_____

_____

_____

_____

_____

_____

"But now, independently of the law, the righteousness of God is tangible and brought to light through Jesus, the Anointed One. This is the righteousness that the Scriptures prophesied would come. It is God's righteousness made visible through the faithfulness of Jesus Christ. And now all who believe in him receive that gift. For there is really no difference between us, for we all have sinned and are in need of the glory of God. Yet through his powerful declaration of acquittal, God freely gives away his righteousness. His gift of love and favor now cascades over us, all because Jesus, the Anointed One, has liberated us from **the guilt, punishment, and power of** sin!" (Romans 3:21-24).

PROVERBS 13

We often underestimate what we carry and bring with us wherever we go. We are called to be Kingdom bringers and can do this by simply carrying righteousness, justice, right standing, peace and joy everywhere that we go. By recognizing the value of what we carry and then sharing it with those around us, we are naturally re-presenting Jesus. We are uniquely and wonderfully made and nobody else can do what is ours to accomplish so let's lean into all that God has made us to be and share it in a manner unique to each of us. There is no shortage of places to bring His Kingdom so let's accept our official role as Kingdom bringers and take seriously the power and authority we have as re-presenters of Christ.

****

Proverbs 13:5-6 – Lovers of God hate what is phony and false, but the wicked are full of shame and behave shamefully. Righteousness is like a shield of protection, guarding those who keep their integrity, but sin is the downfall of the wicked.

****

Proverbs 13:13-25 – Despise the word, will you? Then you'll pay the price and it won't be pretty! But the one who honors the Father's holy instructions will be rewarded. When the lovers of God teach you truth, a fountain of life opens up within you, and their wise instruction will deliver you from the ways of death. Everyone admires a wise, sensible person, but the treacherous walk on the path of ruin. Everything a wise and shrewd man does comes from a source of revelation-knowledge, but the behavior of a fool puts foolishness on parade!

An undependable messenger causes a lot of trouble, but the trustworthy and wise messengers release healing wherever they go. Poverty and disgrace come to the one who refuses to hear criticism. But the one who is easy to correct is on the path of honor. When God fulfills your longings, sweetness fills your soul. But the wicked refuse to turn from darkness *to see their desires come to pass*. If you want to grow in wisdom, spend time with the wise. Walk with the wicked and you'll eventually become just like them.

Calamity chases the sin-chaser, but prosperity pursues the God-lover. The benevolent man leaves an inheritance that endures to his children's children, but the wealth of the wicked is treasured up for the righteous. The lovers of God will live a long life and get to enjoy their wealth, but the ungodly will suddenly perish. If you withhold correction and punishment from your children, you demonstrate a lack of true love. So prove your love and be prompt to punish them. The lovers of God will have more than enough, but the wicked will always lack what they crave.

Declarations

- I am a lover of God.
- I remain true to Him and who He has made me to be.
- I walk in humility and wisdom.
- I agree with all that God says about me.
- His ways work and I work His way. I relay heaven's message everywhere I go, spreading righteousness, peace, and joy in the Holy Spirit.
- I am living a full abundant life because that's what Jesus came to give me – a full abundant life!

My Personal Revelation of Wisdom

_____

_____

_____

_____

_____

My Personal Applications

_____

_____

_____

_____

_____

_____

My Personal Declarations

_____

_____

_____

_____

_____

"For the kingdom of God is not a matter
of rules about food and drink, but is in
the realm of the Holy Spirit, filled with
righteousness, peace, and joy"
(Romans 14:17).

PROVERBS 14

Growing up as the youngest of three girls in a pastor's home, I heard and saw so many different types of people and situations that it was easy to become critical. Any time Dad would hear us start making fun of or criticizing someone, he would say, "Girls, don't you get a critical spirit!" We would laugh and roll our eyes, appeasing his 'old school' ways.

As I got older, that statement has stayed with me along with what I've heard Pastor Bill Johnson say, "We need to learn to value people for who they are, without stumbling over who they are not." This is the foundation to speaking life and bringing hope to others – while keeping us far from what Dad warned us about, which is a critical spirit!

****

Proverbs 14:1-22 – Every wise woman encourages and builds up her family, but a foolish woman over time will tear it down by her own actions. Lovers of truth follow the right path because of their wonderment and worship of God. But the devious display their disdain for him. The words of a proud fool will all come back to haunt him. But the words of the wise will become a shield of protection around them. The only clean stable is an empty stable. So if you want the work of an ox and to enjoy an abundant harvest, you'll have a mess or two to clean up!

An honest witness will never lie, but a deceitful witness lies with every breath. The intellectually arrogant seek for wisdom, but they never seem to discover what they claim they're looking for. For revelation-knowledge flows to the one who hungers for understanding. The words of the wise are like weapons of knowledge. If you need wise counsel, stay away from the fool. For the wisdom of the wise will keep life on the right track while the fool only deceives himself and refuses to face reality.

Fools mock the need for repentance, while the favor of

God rests upon all his lovers. Don't expect anyone else to fully understand both the bitterness and the joys of all you experience in your life. The household of the wicked is soon torn apart, while the family of the righteous flourishes. You can rationalize it all you want and justify the path of error you have chosen, but you'll find out in the end that you took the road to destruction. Superficial laughter can hide a heavy heart, but when the laughter ends, the pain resurfaces.

Those who turn from the truth get what they deserve, but a good person receives a sweet reward. A gullible person will believe anything, but a sensible person will confirm the facts. A wise person is careful in all things and turns quickly from evil, while the impetuous fool moves ahead with overconfidence. An impulsive person has a short fuse and can ruin everything, but the wise show self-control. The naïve demonstrate a lack of wisdom, but the lovers of wisdom are crowned with revelation-knowledge.

Evil ones will pay tribute to good people and eventually come to be servants of the godly. The poor are disliked even by their neighbors, but everyone wants to get close to the wealthy. It's a sin to despise one who is less fortunate than you, but when you are kind to the poor, you will prosper and be blessed. Haven't you noticed how evil schemers always wander astray? But kindness and truth come to those who make plans to be pure in all their ways.

****

Proverbs 14:26-27 – Confidence and strength flood the hearts of the lovers of God who live in awe of him, and their devotion provides their children with a place of shelter and security. To worship God in wonder and awe opens a fountain of life within you, empowering you to escape death's domain.

****

Proverbs 14:29-31 – 29When your heart overflows with understanding you'll be very slow to get angry. But if you have a quick temper, your impatience will be quickly seen by all. 30A tender, tranquil heart will make you healthy, but jealousy can make you sick. 31Insult your Creator, will you? That's exactly what you do every time you oppress the powerless! Showing kindness to the poor is equal to honoring your maker.

Declarations

- I make good decisions because I fear the Lord.
- I am confident of God's help in every situation.
- I accept people for who they are.
- I speak life to those around me.
- I continually depend on Him in every situation.

My Personal Revelation of Wisdom

_____

_____

_____

_____

_____

_____

My Personal Applications

_____

_____

_____

_____

_____

My Personal Declarations

_____

_____

_____

_____

_____

"Yet I was captured by grace, so that
Jesus Christ could display through me the
outpouring of his Spirit as a pattern to be
seen for all those who would believe in
him for eternal life" (1 Timothy 1:16).

PROVERBS 15

"If you can't say something good, don't say anything at all!" I'm sure you've heard this at one time or another, and if you're honest, you'll admit it's not always easy to do. Negativity is like a magnet for the enemy. He is attracted to and loves to get involved in negativity, twisting and magnifying it. When you think of it, nothing that God says about us or to us is negative. In fact nothing about God is negative.

So then, with whom are you going to partner? Will you partner with negativity and the working of our enemy or will you partner with God and all the good positive things that He has planned for you and others?

****

Proverbs 15:1-4 – Respond gently when you are confronted and you'll defuse the rage of another. Responding with sharp, cutting words will only make it worse. Don't you know that being angry can ruin the testimony of even the wisest of men? When wisdom speaks, understanding becomes attractive. But the words of the fool make their ignorance look laughable. The eyes of the Lord are everywhere and he takes note of everything that happens. He watches over his lovers, and he also sees the wickedness of the wicked. When you speak healing words, you offer others fruit from the tree of life. But unhealthy, negative words do nothing but crush their hopes.

****

Proverbs 15:13-33 – A cheerful heart puts a smile on your face, but a broken heart leads to depression. Lovers of God hunger after truth, but those without understanding feast on foolishness and don't even realize it. Everything seems to go wrong when you feel weak and depressed. But when you choose to be cheerful, every day will bring you more and more joy and fullness. It's much better to live simply, surrounded in holy awe and worship of God, than to have great wealth with a home full of trouble.

Wisdom Declarations

It's much better to have a meal of vegetables surrounded with love and grace than a steak where there is hate. A touchy, hot-tempered man picks a fight, but the calm, patient man knows how to silence strife. Nothing seems to work right for the lazy man, but life seems smooth and easy when your heart is virtuous. When a son learns wisdom, a father's heart is glad. But the man who shames his mother is a foolish son. The senseless fool treats life like a joke, but the one with living-understanding makes good choices.

Your plans will fall apart right in front of you if you fail to get good advice. But if you first seek out multiple counselors, you'll watch your plans succeed. Everyone enjoys giving great advice. But how delightful it is to say the right thing at the right time! The life-paths of the prudent lift them progressively heavenward, delivering them from the death spirals that keep tugging them downward. The Lord champions the widow's cause, but watch him as he smashes down the houses of the haughty!

The Lord detests wicked ways of thinking, but he enjoys lovely and delightful words. The one who puts earning money above his family will have trouble at home, but those who refuse to exploit others will live *in peace*. Lovers of God think before they speak, but the careless blurt out wicked words meant to cause harm. The Lord doesn't respond to the wicked, but he's moved to answer the prayers of the righteous. Eyes that focus on what is beautiful bring joy to the heart, and hearing a good report refreshes and strengthens the inner being.

Accepting constructive criticism opens your heart to the path of life, making you right at home among the wise. Refusing constructive criticism shows you have no interest in improving your life, for revelation-insight only comes as you accept correction and the wisdom that it brings. The source of revelation-knowledge is found as you fall down in surrender before the Lord. Don't expect to see Shekinah glory until the Lord sees your sincere humility.

Declarations

- The words that I speak matter.
- I speak life and answer gently.
- I let love lead my thoughts and my words. Love is leading my life.
- Love empowers me to live in humility and the increased awareness and acknowledgment of Gods' working in my life.

My Personal Revelation of Wisdom

_____

_____

_____

_____

_____

_____

My Personal Applications

_____

_____

_____

_____

_____

My Personal Declarations

_____

_____

_____

_____

_____

"He offers a resting place for me in his luxurious love. His tracks take me to an oasis of peace near the quiet brook of bliss" (Psalms 23:2).

PROVERBS 16

We were attending Bible College in Joplin, MO when my husband Ted proposed. Once the semester ended, I went to live with my parents in Northwest Arkansas to prepare for a wedding. Once we chose the date, we needed to figure out where we would live after we were married. Should we go to Joplin where Ted lived, or should we live in Northwest Arkansas? We decided to go the "super spiritual" route of whoever got the best first fulltime job would determine where we lived. So, we both started looking for employment and praying God would lead us.

I thought for sure that Ted would find the better job more quickly than I, but I tried my best anyway. A job came up that I really wanted, one that I thought I could be good at. However, I felt under qualified and it also required me to be 18 (I was only 17), so I put my start date for one day after my birthday and decided to trust God. I couldn't believe it when I was asked to come in for an interview. I was so nervous and scared that I almost talked myself out of going since I assumed I wouldn't get it anyway. I thought the interview went well but truthfully I had never interviewed for a job of this caliber before. I was shocked and amazed when two days later I received a phone call that I had gotten the job! I was going to work for Walmart Corporate Office Pharmacy Division as the assistant to the regional manager.

I called Ted and told him I got the job, and he was so excited that he began to look for jobs in the same region. Within a week or so, Ted had an interview at Sam's Club Corporate Offices and got a great job with them. We would be working literally down the street from each other. This was the start of our life together and we knew we were exactly where God wanted us to be. We were able to support my parents in their new venture of planting a church and would soon be working with them in full-time church ministry.

We had trusted God and He had led us in the exact path He had for each of us. If He did that for us, I know He will do that for you too – keep seeking Him and keep on trusting Him. He is your faithful Father.

****

Proverbs 16:1-9 – Go ahead and make all the plans you want, but it's the Lord who will ultimately direct your steps. We are all in love with our own opinions, convinced they're correct. But the Lord is in the midst of us, testing and probing our every motive. Before you do anything, put your trust totally in God and not in yourself. Then every plan you make will succeed. The Lord works everything together to accomplish his purpose. Even the wicked are included in his plans—he sets them aside for the day of disaster. Yahweh detests all the proud of heart, for pride attracts his punishment—and you can count on that!

You can avoid evil through surrendered worship and the fear of God, for the power of his faithful love removes sin's guilt and grip over you. When the Lord is pleased with the decisions you've made, he activates grace to turn enemies into friends. It is better to have little with a heart that loves justice than to be rich and not have God on your side. Within your heart you can make plans for your future, but the Lord chooses the steps you take to get there.

****

Proverbs 16:17-26 – Repenting from evil places you on the highway of holiness. Protect purity and you protect your life. Your boast becomes a prophecy of a future failure. The higher you lift yourself up in pride, the harder you'll fall in disgrace. It's better to be meek and lowly and live among the poor than to live high and mighty among the rich and famous. One skilled in business discovers prosperity, but the one who trusts in God is blessed beyond belief! The one with a wise heart is called "discerning," and speaking sweetly to others makes your teaching even more convincing.

Wisdom is a deep well of understanding opened up within you as a fountain of life for others, but it's senseless to try to instruct a fool. Winsome words pour from a heart of wisdom, adding value to all you teach. Nothing is more appealing than speaking beautiful, life-giving words. For they release sweetness to our souls and inner healing to our spirits. Before every person there is a path that seems like the right one to take, but it leads straight to hell! Life motivation comes from the deep longings of the heart, and the passion to see them fulfilled urges you onward.

****

Proverbs 16:32-33 – Do you want to be a mighty warrior? It's better to be known as one who is patient and slow to anger. Do you want to conquer a city? Rule over your temper before you attempt to rule a city. We may toss the coin and roll the dice, but God's will is greater than luck.

Declarations

- I make plans and trust the Lord to direct each step.
- Before I do anything, I put my trust in Him.
- God is working everything together for my good and His purposes.
- His grace is sufficient for me and His strength is made perfect in my weakness.
- His love never fails.
- As I protect my purity, I am protecting my life.
- God sets the standard that I live by, and His blessings and goodness overtake me.
- I love to hear godly, truthful counsel.
- I seek wisdom and cultivate a heart of understanding. Repentance, changing the way I think, positions me to be all that God has designed me to be.
- I am created on purpose for a purpose!

My Personal Revelation of Wisdom

_____

_____

_____

_____

_____

My Personal Applications

_____

_____

_____

_____

_____

My Personal Declarations

_____

_____

_____

_____

_____

"Trust in the Lord completely, and do not rely on your own opinions. With all your heart rely on him to guide you, and he will lead you in every decision you make" (Proverbs 3:5).

PROVERBS 17

Nothing is wasted in God, not our effort, our suffering, our prayers, and even our seeming failures. I don't know how God does it, but somehow and someway God takes everything we have been through, everything we have learned and accomplished, and works them together for our good and His glory! Trusting this truth no matter what we are going through is quite important for our growth because it keeps us open to what He is actually doing. It keeps us trusting in Him and depending upon Him. You might have a degree you're not using or a career path that you are no longer on and you have thought that those years were wasted. I want to remind you that nothing is wasted! God is working it all out for your good and His glory! Keep going and keep growing.

****

Proverbs 17:1-3 – A simple, humble life with peace and quiet is far better than an opulent lifestyle with nothing but quarrels and strife at home. A wise, intelligent servant will be honored above a shameful son. He'll even end up having a portion left to him in his master's will. In the same way that gold and silver are refined by fire, the Lord purifies your heart by the tests and trials of life.

****

Proverbs 17:8-10 – Wise instruction is like a costly gem. It turns the impossible into success. Love overlooks the mistakes of others, but dwelling on the failures of others devastates friendships. One word of correction breaks open a teachable heart, but a fool can be corrected a hundred times and still not know what hit him.

****

Proverbs 17:22 – A joyful, cheerful heart brings healing to both body and soul. But the one whose heart is crushed struggles with sickness and depression.

****

Proverbs 17:26-28 – It's horrible to persecute a holy lover

of God or to strike an honorable man for his integrity! Can you bridle your tongue when your heart is under pressure? That's how you show that you are wise. An understanding heart keeps you cool, calm, and collected, no matter what you're facing. When even a fool bites his tongue he's considered wise. So shut your mouth when you are provoked—it will make you look smart.

Declarations

- I live in peace and humility, simply loving and trusting Jesus.
- He is working all things out for my good.
- I see that everything I'm going through I am *growing* through.
- I treat others how I want to be treated, valuing them for who they are without stumbling over who they are not.
- I value people.
- I love people.
- My heart is cheerful, joyful and understanding and my words follow my heart.

My Personal Revelation of Wisdom

_____

_____

_____

_____

My Personal Applications

_____

_____

_____

_____

_____

My Personal Declarations

_____

_____

_____

_____

_____

"So we are convinced that every detail of our lives is continually woven together for good, for we are his lovers who have been called to fulfill his designed purpose" (Romans 8:28).

PROVERBS 18

My children were four, two and six months old when I found myself on my hands and knees scrubbing the toilet and griping to God. I was letting Him have it: "All I do is clean and cook and do laundry and change diapers and clean up throw-up along with all the other messes. I am supposed to be doing things for You and here I am in the throes of motherhood, stuck cleaning up after everybody else! When do I get to do Your work?"

I still remember so vividly the still small voice of my Jesus saying, "Tami, everything you do, do it as unto me!" I stopped scrubbing and turned my toilet into an altar, asking for forgiveness for my shortsightedness and small-mindedness. I then began to thank Him for my children and my husband and our home and all He provided for us. By the time I was finished praying, that bathroom was cleaner than it ever had been! It was then that I realized my whole life was meant to be an offering of worship to Him!

****

Proverbs 18:1-4 – An unfriendly person isolates himself and seems to care only about his own issues. For his contempt of sound judgment makes him a recluse. Senseless people find no pleasure in acquiring true wisdom, for all they want to do is impress you with what they know. An ungodly man is always cloaked with disgrace, as dishonor and shame are his companions. Words of wisdom are like a fresh, flowing brook— like deep waters that spring forth from within, bubbling up inside the one with understanding.

****

Proverbs 18:9-15 – The one who is too lazy to look for work is the same one who wastes his life away. The character of God is a tower of strength, for the lovers of God delight to run into his heart and be exalted on high. The rich, in their conceit, imagine that their wealth is enough to protect them. It becomes their confidence in a day of trouble. A man's heart is the proudest when his downfall is nearest, for he won't see glory until the Lord sees humility. Listen before you speak, for to speak before you've heard the facts will bring humiliation. The will to live sustains you when you're sick, but depression crushes courage and leaves you unable to cope. The spiritually hungry are always ready to learn more, for their hearts are eager to discover new truths.

****

Proverbs 18:20-21 – Sharing words of wisdom is satisfying to your inner being. It encourages you to know that you've changed someone else's life. Your words are so powerful that they will kill or give life, and the talkative person will reap the consequences.

****

Proverbs 18:24 – Some friendships don't last for long, but there is one loving friend who is joined to your heart closer than any other!

Declarations

- I am a hard worker.
- Everything that I do is for the Lord.
- His name is my strong tower that provides me with safety and refuge.
- I run to Him and trust Him completely!
- I am thankful for my family and friends.
- I am humble in heart and not easily offended.
- My giftings from the Lord make a place for me.
- My words bring light and life.

My Personal Revelation of Wisdom

My Personal Applications

_____

_____

_____

_____

_____

_____

My Personal Declarations

_____

_____

_____

_____

_____

"Always give thanks to Father God for
every person he brings into your life
in the name of our Lord Jesus Christ"
(Ephesians 5:20).

PROVERBS 19

I sometimes find it quite humorous when I consider the plans we have made over the years. As newlyweds, we had a five-year plan to start a family. I was pregnant three months into our marriage. In our first eighteen months of marriage, we moved, built a house, changed careers, had a baby, and lost another baby. None of this was in our five-year plan, let alone our 18-month plan.

Having a plan is good but God's plans are always better. The key to this is always holding our plans loosely, for they are not always going to turn out how we described them, but we can count on God to lead us in the way we need to go. He is always there to see us through and work it out for our good. I do not have the answer as to why I lost our second child but I do know that the Holy Spirit showed Himself strong as my comforter and I had the privilege of knowing, seeing and experiencing God in a new way. I also learned how to start trusting God with the "big question marks" in my life. This is proving to be a valuable lesson for me up to the present day. I don't need to know the answer to my many why questions, but I have learned I need to trust and lean into Him. Blessed are the flexible for they shall not be broken.

****

Proverbs 19:1-3 – It's better to be honest, even if it leads to poverty, than to live as a dishonest fool. The best way to live is with revelation-knowledge, for without it, you'll grow impatient and run right into error. There are some people who ruin their own lives and then blame it all on God.

****

Proverbs 19:8 – Do yourself a favor and love wisdom. Learn all you can, then watch your life flourish and prosper!

****

Proverbs 19:11 – An understanding person demonstrates patience, for mercy means holding your tongue. When you are insulted, be quick to forgive and forget it, for you are virtuous when you overlook an offense.

****

Wisdom Declarations

Proverbs 19:15-23 – Go ahead—be lazy and passive. But you'll go hungry if you live that way. Honor God's holy instructions and life will go well for you. But if you despise his ways and choose your own plans, you will die. Every time you give to the poor you make a loan to the Lord. Don't worry—you'll be repaid in full for all the good you've done. Don't be afraid to discipline your children while they're still young enough to learn. Don't indulge your children or be swayed by their protests.

A hot-tempered man has to pay the price for his anger. If you bail him out once, you'll do it a dozen times. Listen well to wise counsel and be willing to learn from correction so that by the end of your life you'll be known for your wisdom. A person may have many ideas concerning God's plan for his life, but only the designs of God's purpose will succeed in the end. A man is charming when he displays tender mercies to others. And a lover of God who is poor and promises nothing is better than a rich liar who never keeps his promises. When you live a life of abandoned love, surrendered before the awe of God, here's what you'll experience: Abundant life. Continual protection. And complete satisfaction!

Declarations

- I am living in the fear of the Lord, receiving all the promises that go along with having a greater awareness, acknowledgment, awe, and respect of Him.
- Integrity and truth are my way of life.
- I am kind to others, practicing the ways of Jesus.
- When I give to the poor, I lend to the Lord!
- My plans are good, but God's plans for me are better.
- I am hungry for wisdom and by keeping understanding, I find all that is good.
- Discretion and grace keep me level-headed and big-hearted.
- I am growing and learning more every day!

My Personal Revelation of Wisdom

_____

_____

_____

_____

_____

My Personal Applications

_____

_____

_____

_____

_____

My Personal Declarations

_____

_____

_____

_____

_____

"Then we will no longer be immature like children. We won't be tossed and blown about by every wind of new teaching. We will not be influenced when people try to trick us with lies so clever they sound like the truth. Instead, we will speak the truth in love, growing in every way more and more like Christ, who is the head of his body, the church. He makes the whole body fit together perfectly. As each part does its own special work, it helps the other parts grow, so that the whole body is healthy and growing and full of love" (Ephesians 4:14-16, NLT).

PROVERBS 20

In the year 2000, Ted and I felt an urgency to get our finances in order. We went to see a financial counselor and came up with a plan to pay off our debt. Part of this process was creating a spending plan and using a cash envelope system for our weekly spending (for everything other than our bills). This was such a useful practice so we could learn to be more disciplined by knowing exactly how much we were spending on eating out, shopping, etc. This actually became fun for us to see how little we could spend from what we planned and put some extra money in a "vacation" envelope.

I was shocked how fast the extra money added up. During this time, we were able to pay off our car and other small debts, and have money to take a small vacation to see Ted's family in Texas. What we did not know was that in 2001 God would reposition us to another assignment that would require big steps of faith. This move would not have been possible if our finances were not in order. We have found that one obedient response opens the door and prepares the way for another.

****

Proverbs 20:4-7 – If you're too lazy to plant seed, it's too bad when you have no harvest on which to feed. A man of deep understanding will give good advice, drawing it out from the well within. Many will tell you they're your loyal friends, but who can find one who is truly trustworthy? The lovers of God will walk in integrity, and their children are fortunate to have godly parents as their examples.

****

Proverbs 20:12-15 – Lovers of God have been given eyes to see and ears to hear from God. If you spend all your time sleeping, you'll grow poor. So wake up, sleepyhead! Don't sleep on the job. And then there will be plenty of food on your table. The buyer says, as he haggles over the price, "That's junk. It's worthless!" Then he goes out and brags, "Look at the great bargain I got!" You may have an abundance of wealth, piles of gold and jewels, but there is something of far greater worth: speaking revelation-words of knowledge.

Wisdom Declarations

****

Proverbs 20:21-30 – If an inheritance is gained too early in life, it will not be blessed in the end. Don't ever say, "I'm going to get even with them if it's the last thing I do!" Wrap God's grace around your heart and he will be the one to vindicate you. The Lord hates double standards—that's hypocrisy at its worst! It is the Lord who directs your life, for each step you take is ordained by God to bring you closer to your destiny. So much of your life, then, remains a mystery!

Be careful in making a rash promise before God, or you may be trapped by your vow and live to regret it. A wise king is able to discern corruption and remove wickedness from his kingdom. The spirit God breathed into man is like a living lamp, a shining light searching into the innermost chamber of our being. Good leadership is built on love and truth, for kindness and integrity are what keep leaders in their position of trust. We admire the young for their strength and beauty, but the dignity of the old is their wisdom. When you are punished severely, you learn your lesson well—for painful experiences do wonders to change your life.

Declarations

- I abide in Jesus which keeps me from striving in my own efforts and with other people.
- Money management is important to me because it's important to God.
- I am a good steward of all that God has provided for me and my family.
- My stewardship, integrity, and generosity benefit generations to come.
- Everything I do is a seed and produces a harvest after its kind.
- I am intentional to plant good seed in order to reap a good harvest.
- Safety and security are my promises from God and He keeps His promises. I am safe. I am secure. I am His.

My Personal Revelation of Wisdom

_____

_____

_____

_____

_____

My Personal Applications

_____

_____

_____

_____

_____

_____

My Personal Declarations

_____

_____

_____

_____

_____

_____

"Yes, God is more than ready to overwhelm you with every form of grace, so that you will have more than enough of everything —every moment and in every way. He will make you overflow with abundance in every good thing you do" (2 Corinthians 9:8).

PROVERBS 21

Once we took the step of faith in 2001, we began to see the supernatural provision of God in ways that we never thought possible. This is when I learned that God is my source and He provides resources from all different places. Once, we received an unexpected bonus that we used for a down payment on a house. We had a family offer to pay for our oldest son to go to a private school (for which I had been asking the Lord). One Christmas, we were invited to a "Happy Birthday Jesus" party by a family in the church that we hadn't known very long.

Honestly, my attitude was very poor. I went to fulfill an obligation and get out of there to be home with my family. Once we stayed as long as was polite, Ted began to get the kids loaded in the van while at the same time the party host asked to speak with me privately in her bedroom. I thought maybe she wanted me to pray for her or something like that. Before I knew it, she had her check book out and as she was writing two checks. She explained to me that her and her husband had come into some money and they wanted to bless our church and us personally. She handed me the checks, hugged me, and said Merry Christmas!

On the way out of the house, I was asking God to forgive me for my attitude and selfishness. I just knew that God used this resource to provide for our needs and I didn't even look at the checks. Once I got in the van, I told Ted what had happened and handed him the checks. The one for the church was for $40,000 and the one for us was for $10,000. I was speechless at the goodness of God. He truly is able to do exceedingly more than what we can ask think or imagine.

****

Proverbs 21:1-5 – It's as easy for God to steer a king's heart for his purposes as it is for him to direct the course of a stream. We may think we're right all the time, but God thoroughly examines our motives. It pleases God more when we demonstrate godliness and justice than when we merely offer him a sacrifice. Arrogance, superiority, and pride are the fruits of sin. Brilliant ideas pay off and bring you prosperity, but making hasty, impatient decisions will only lead to financial loss.

****

Proverbs 21:11-13 – Senseless people learn their lessons the hard way, but the wise are teachable. A godly, righteous person has the ability to bring the light of instruction to the wicked even though he despises what the wicked do. If you close your heart to the cries of the poor, then I'll close my ears when you cry out to me!

****

Proverbs 21:20-31 – In wisdom's house you'll find delightful treasures and the oil of the Holy Spirit. But the stupid squander what they've been given. The lovers of God who chase after righteousness will find all their dreams come true: an abundant life drenched with favor and a fountain that overflows with satisfaction. A warrior filled with wisdom ascends into the high place and releases breakthrough, bringing down the strongholds of the mighty. Watch your words and be careful what you say, and you'll be surprised by how few troubles you'll have. An arrogant man is inflated with pride—nothing but a snooty scoffer in love with his own opinion. Mr. Mocker is his name!

Taking the easy way out is the habit of a lazy man, and it will be his downfall. All day long he thinks about all the things that he craves, for he hasn't learned the secret that the generous man has learned: extravagant giving never leads to poverty. To bring an offering to God with an ulterior motive is detestable, for it amounts to nothing but hypocrisy. No one believes a notorious liar, but the guarded words of an honest man stand the test of time. The wicked are shameless and stubborn, but the lovers of God have a holy confidence. All your brilliant wisdom and clever insight will be of no help at all if the Lord is against you. You can do your best to prepare for the battle, but ultimate victory comes from the Lord God.

Declarations

- The Lord directs my heart in the way that I should go.
- I am well loved.
- I follow His righteousness and mercy and in return find life, righteousness, and honor.
- My way is established and secure because Jesus is the Way.
- I am in Him and He is in me!
- Safety and security are my promises from God and He keeps His promises. I am safe. I am secure. I am His.

My Personal Revelation of Wisdom

_____

_____

_____

_____

_____

_____

My Personal Applications

_____

_____

_____

_____

_____

My Personal Declarations

_____

_____

_____

_____

_____

"No matter what, I will continue to hope and passionately cling to Christ, so that he will be openly revealed through me before everyone's eyes. So I will not be ashamed! In my life or in my death, Christ will be magnified in me" (Philippians 1:20).

PROVERBS 22

I love the story of Daniel in the Old Testament to see how God positioned him and gave him favor to serve underneath a wicked ruler while serving God wholeheartedly. This was not without trial, for if you remember, he was thrown into the lions' den and watched his three friends get thrown into the fiery furnace. This was also not without supernatural intervention by the miraculous hand and favor of God.

Favor is not the absence of trial or hardship. Look at Mary, the mother of Jesus, and Jesus himself. Living in the favor of God means you live assured that He is with you and will bring you through anything that comes your way. In the process, your life re-presents Him and manifests how well He takes care of His children.

****

Proverbs 22:1-4 – A beautiful reputation is more to be desired than great riches, and to be esteemed by others is more honorable than to own immense investments. The rich and the poor have one thing in common: the Lord God created each one. A prudent person with insight foresees danger coming and prepares himself for it. But the senseless rush blindly forward and suffer the consequences. Laying your life down in tender surrender before the Lord will bring life, prosperity, and honor as your reward.

****

Proverbs 22:8-12 – Sin is a seed that brings a harvest; you'll reap a heap of trouble with every seed you plant. For your investment in sins pays a full return—the full punishment you deserve! When you are generous to the poor, you are enriched with blessings in return. Say goodbye to a troublemaker and you'll say goodbye to quarrels, strife, tension, and arguments, for a troublemaker traffics in shame. The Lord loves those whose hearts are holy, and he is the friend of those whose ways are pure.

God passionately watches over his deep reservoir of revelation-knowledge, but he subverts the lies of those who pervert the truth.

****

Proverbs 22:17-29 – Listen carefully and open your heart. Drink in the wise revelation that I impart. You'll become winsome and wise when you treasure the beauty of my words. And always be prepared to share them at the appropriate time. For I'm releasing these words to you this day, yes, even to you, so that your living hope will be found in God alone, for he is the only one who is always true.

Pay attention to these excellent sayings of three-fold things. For within my words you will discover true and reliable revelation. They will give you serenity so that you can reveal the truth of the word of the one who sends you. Never oppress the poor or pass laws with the motive of crushing the weak. For the Lord will rise to plead their case and humiliate the one who humiliates the poor. Walk away from an angry man or you'll embrace a snare in your soul by becoming bad-tempered just like him.

Why would you ever guarantee a loan for someone else or promise to be responsible for someone's debts? For if you fail to pay you could lose your shirt! The previous generation has set boundaries in place. Don't you dare move them just to benefit yourself. If you are uniquely gifted in your work, you will rise and be promoted. You won't be held back—you'll stand before kings!

Declarations

- I live in the favor of God.
- I am His creation and I exhibit His creative power every day.
- Everything is a seed that produces after its own kind. I choose to plant humility, love, generosity, purity, and kindness with my heart-felt words and actions.
- With the help of Holy Spirit, I am faithful and diligent, working hard and excelling at everything I do.
- I tune my ear to Him and apply my heart to understanding His ways.
- I live in the loving favor of God!
- Safety and security are my promises from God and He keeps His promises. I am safe. I am secure. I am His.

My Personal Revelation of Wisdom

_____

_____

_____

_____

_____

My Personal Applications

_____

_____

_____

_____

_____

_____

My Personal Declarations

_____

_____

_____

_____

_____

_____

"The seed that fell into good, fertile soil represents those lovers of truth who hear it deep within their hearts. They respond by clinging to the word, keeping it dear as they endure all things in faith. This is the seed that will one day bear much fruit in their lives" (Luke 8:15).

PROVERBS 23

There is good reason that every car on the road has a windshield that is bigger than the rearview mirror. The same goes for how we live our lives. At times it is tempting to look to the past and wish we could go back to "the good ol' days." However, there are a few things about the past that we need to keep in mind. The first is that we can't change anything that has already happened. It is a massive waste of time living in the shoulda-coulda-woulda of the past.

Second, we have already been there and done that. Why do we want to repeat what has already been done? Even if they were good times, do we truly believe that they were the only good time that can ever be had? Third, living in and idolizing the past prevents us from truly living today. We can't move forward while looking back without stumbling over what is right in front of us.

What has helped me the most where this is concerned is to give God thanks for all He has done and for all that He is planning to do. We do not honor those who have gone before us by trying to relive what they have already accomplished. We honor them by viewing their ceiling as our floor. We don't have shoes to fill but a floor to dance on! By taking the principles of what they have taught us and applying them to our circumstances now, we are looking through our windshield with a glance of gratitude in our rearview mirror.

****

Proverbs 23:10-25 – Never move a long-standing boundary line or attempt to take land that belongs to the fatherless. For they have a mighty protector, a loving redeemer, who watches over them, and he will stand up for their cause. Pay close attention to the teaching that corrects you, and open your heart to every word of instruction. Don't withhold appropriate discipline from your child. Go ahead and punish him when he needs it. Don't worry—it won't kill him! A good spanking could be the very thing that teaches him a lifelong lesson! My beloved child, when your heart is full of wisdom, my heart is full of gladness. 16And when you speak anointed words, we are speaking mouth to mouth!

Don't allow the actions of evil men to cause you to burn with anger. Instead, burn with unrelenting passion as you worship God in holy awe. Your future is bright and filled with a living hope that will never fade away. As you listen to me, my beloved child, you will grow in wisdom and your heart will be drawn into understanding, which will empower you to make right decisions. Don't live in the excesses of drunkenness or gluttony, or waste your life away by partying all the time, because drunkards and gluttons sleep their lives away and end up broke!

Give respect to your father and mother for without them you wouldn't even be here. And don't neglect them when they grow old. Embrace the truth and hold it close. Don't let go of wisdom, instruction, and life-giving understanding. When a father observes his child living in godliness, he is ecstatic with joy—nothing makes him prouder! So may your father's heart burst with joy and your mother's soul be filled with gladness because of you.

Declarations

- I honor the past while looking forward to the future.
- My hope is in the Lord.
- I set my mind and heart on what He says about me.
- I am His child. I am blessed with the purpose to bless others.
- My heart and ears are applied to His word so that I can put it to action.
- My hope is in the Lord and my future is secure.

My Personal Revelation of Wisdom

_____

_____

_____

_____

_____

My Personal Applications

_____

_____

_____

_____

_____

My Personal Declarations

_____

_____

_____

_____

_____

"I don't depend on my own strength to
accomplish this; however I do have one
compelling focus: I forget all of the past
as I fasten my heart to the future instead"
(Philippians 3:13).

PROVERBS 24

1 Timothy 1:18 says, "This charge I commit to you, son Timothy, according to the prophecies previously made concerning you, that by them you may wage the good warfare." Paul was admonishing Timothy and us as well to fight our battles with the prophecies we have received. Our oldest son, Zach had been a prodigal for almost 10 years. Through the years, the Lord had encouraged and spoken to me at different times regarding our prodigal; how to pray for him or things to do and not do for him. However, this was the first time I had received a prophetic word specifically about Zach, and it was from a total stranger.

On this particular Sunday, I was feeling hurt and discouraged. I was weary. As we were walking into church one of the greeters followed me to my seat telling me that they felt they had a word from the Lord and asked if I knew anyone named Daniel. Zach's middle name is Daniel, so I immediately responded with open ears to what the Lord would want to say. She proceeded to tell me that before Zach's birthday, he would humble himself and the Lord would turn his heart to gold.

Between January and May, my husband and I waged the good spiritual fight with our word from the Lord and I am excited to report that on May 29th one day before Zach's twenty-seventh birthday he showed up on our doorstep wanting and ready to get help! This was the beginning of Zach's recovery and total restoration.

Whether you are holding on to a promise from the written Word or a prophetic word, rest assured that God's Word never returns void and there is nothing that is too big for Him. He is faithful to complete what He has started. Take hold of His promises and fight the good fight of faith today and every day.

****

Proverbs 24:3-22 – Wise people are builders—they build families, businesses, communities. And through intelligence and insight their enterprises are established and endure. Because of their skilled leadership, the hearts of people are filled with the treasures of wisdom and the pleasures of spiritual wealth. Wisdom can make anyone into a mighty warrior, and revelation-knowledge increases strength. Wise strategy is necessary to wage war, and with many astute advisers you'll see the path to victory more clearly.

Wisdom is a treasure too lofty for a quarreling fool—he'll have nothing to say when leaders gather together. There is one who makes plans to do evil—Master Schemer is his name. If you plan to do evil, it's as wrong as doing it. And everyone detests a troublemaker. If you faint when under pressure, you have need of courage. Go and rescue the perishing! Be their savior! Why would you stand back and watch them stagger to their death?

And why would you say, "But it's none of my business"? The one who knows you completely and judges your every motive is also the keeper of souls—and not just yours! He sees through your excuses and holds you responsible for failing to help those whose lives are threatened. Revelation-knowledge is a delicacy, sweet like flowing honey that melts in your mouth. Eat as much of it as you can, my friend! For then you will perceive what is true wisdom, your future will be bright, and this hope living within you will never disappoint you.

Listen up, you wicked, irreverent ones—don't harass the lovers of God and don't invade their resting place. For the lovers of God may suffer adversity and stumble seven times, but they will continue to rise over and over again. But the unrighteous are brought down by just one calamity *and will never be able to rise again*. Never gloat when your enemy meets disaster, and don't be quick to rejoice if he falls. For the Lord, who sees your heart, will be displeased with you and will pity your foe.

Don't be angrily offended over evildoers or be agitated by them. For the wicked have no life and no future—their light of life will die out. My child, stand in awe of Yahweh! Give counsel to others, but don't mingle with those who are rebellious. For sudden destruction will fall upon them and their lives will be ruined in a moment. And who knows what retribution they will face!

****

Proverbs 24:26-27 – Speaking honestly is a sign of true friendship. Go ahead, build your career and give yourself to your work. But if you put me first, you'll see your family built up!

****

Proverbs 24:33-34 – Professional work habits prevent poverty from becoming your permanent business partner. And: If you put off until tomorrow the work you could do today, tomorrow never seems to come.

Declarations

- Jesus is perfect wisdom.
- Jesus builds my life and establishes my future in Himself.
- His strength is made perfect in my weakness.
- In Him, I get back up and rise anytime I stumble.
- In Him, I find forgiveness and the ability to give forgiveness to others, treating them how I want to be treated.
- I am free to dream and accomplish all He has purposed for me to be and do.
- I am His handiwork, purposed for good works that glorify Him.

My Personal Revelation of Wisdom

_____

_____

_____

_____

_____

My Personal Applications

_____

_____

_____

_____

_____

_____

My Personal Declarations

_____

_____

_____

_____

_____

_____

"But he answered me, "My grace is always more than enough for you, and my power finds its full expression through your weakness." So I will celebrate my weaknesses, for when I'm weak I sense more deeply the mighty power of Christ living in me" (2 Corinthians 12:9).

PROVERBS 25

Our spiritual formation is our responsibility. Unfortunately our church culture has created an expectation that a local church should feed us but we must be self-feeders. When we come together to worship corporately, we are celebrating all God has done in our lives while also enjoying fellowship and celebrating community with other believers which provides support and help. We also receive a corporate word to apply to our day-to-day lives as a supplement to what God is already providing for us individually.

One of my favorite practices for my spiritual formation is what I refer to as relational learning, which is learning through an intimate relationship with Jesus, the Father, and the Holy Spirit. Relational learning differs from study. Study time is equally important when we dig into the Word, learning what it says so we can apply it to our lives. Relational learning is conversing with the Father, Son, and Holy Spirit, asking questions, worshiping, and taking time to listen. Relational learning can happen throughout our day and in our quiet times. We may even choose to remember in those times what Jesus did for us through His life, death and resurrection by taking personal communion. Intentionally setting time aside to get to know the Lord is a important part of our relational learning journey and spiritual formation.

****

Proverbs 25:2-16 – God conceals the revelation of his word in the hiding place of his glory. But the honor of kings is revealed by how they thoroughly search out the deeper meaning of all that God says. The heart of a king is full of understanding, like the heavens are high and the ocean is deep. If you burn away the impurities from silver, a sterling vessel will emerge from the fire. And if you purge corruption from the kingdom, a king's reign will be established in righteousness.

Don't boast in the presence of a king or promote yourself by taking a seat at the head table and pretending that you're someone important. For it is better for the king to say to you, "Come, you should sit at the head table," than for him to say in front of everyone, "Please get up and move—you're sitting in the place of the prince." Don't be hasty to file a lawsuit. By starting something you wish you hadn't, you could be humiliated when you lose your case. Don't reveal another person's secret just to prove a point in an argument, or you could be accused of being a gossip 10and gain a reputation for being one who betrays the confidence of a friend.

Winsome words spoken at just the right time are as appealing as apples gilded in gold surrounded with silver. When you humbly receive wise correction, it adorns your life with beauty and makes you a better person. A reliable, trustworthy messenger refreshes the heart of his master, like a gentle snowfall at harvest time. Clouds that carry no water and a wind that brings no refreshing rain—that's what you're like when you boast of a gift that you don't have. Use patience and kindness when you want to persuade leaders and watch them change their minds right in front of you. For your gentle wisdom will quell the strongest resistance. When you discover something sweet, don't overindulge and eat more than you need, for excess in anything can make you sick of even a good thing.

****

Proverbs 25:21-28 – Is your enemy hungry? Buy him lunch. Win him over with your kindness. Your surprising generosity will awaken his conscience and God will reward you with favor. As the north wind brings a storm, saying things you shouldn't brings a storm to any relationship. It's better to live all alone in a rundown shack than to share a castle with a crabby spouse!

Like a drink of cool water refreshes a weary, thirsty soul, so hearing good news revives the spirit. When a lover of God gives in and compromises with wickedness, it can be compared to contaminating a stream with sewage or polluting a fountain. It's good to eat sweet things, but you can take too much. It's good to be honored, but to seek words of praise is not honor at all. If you live without restraint and are unable to control your temper, you're as helpless as a city with broken-down defenses, open to attack.

Declarations

- God hides things for me not from me.
- I choose to seek Him and His ways, learning and growing every day.
- My words are powerful and the Holy Spirit helps me speak the truth with love.
- The Holy Spirit gives me discretion and discernment to know what to say and when to say it so my words are effective, encouraging, and appropriately beautiful.
- Generosity and forgiveness are my way of life.
- God-confidence empowers me to prefer others before myself.
- I am responsible for my spiritual formation.
- I am growing more and more to be like Jesus.
- I encourage myself in the Word and apply it to me life.
- I am who He (Jesus) says I am!

My Personal Revelation of Wisdom

_____

_____

_____

_____

_____

_____

My Personal Applications

_____

_____

_____

_____

_____

_____

My Personal Declarations

_____

_____

_____

_____

_____

_____

"He's the hope that holds me and the stronghold to shelter me, the only God for me, and my great confidence"
(Psalms 91:2).

PROVERBS 26

People have heard me say that I am un-offendable. This doesn't mean that I haven't been wronged or that I haven't had to work through offense, I definitely have and will continue to do so. What it does mean is that I am practicing premeditated forgiveness. Forgiveness should not only be part of what we do but also become who we are.

We are forgiven people; it is a significant part of our identity. So if we are living forgiven, then giving forgiveness emanates from who we truly are. We are simply sharing what Jesus has so graciously given us. When we find ourselves struggling to forgive, we must remember that holding on to unforgiveness is detrimental to our spiritual formation and health as well as our physical bodies. It is not harmful to those who have wronged, but is toxic behavior for us. Holding on to our offenses is a strategy of the enemy that keeps us from living in our true identity in Christ. Forgiveness received and given brings freedom, peace, and joy. Let's practice premeditated forgiveness.

****

Proverbs 26:1-19 – It is totally out of place to promote and honor a fool, just like it's out of place to have snow in the summer and rain at harvest time. An undeserved curse will be powerless to harm you. It may flutter over you like a bird, but it will find no place to land. Guide a horse with a whip, direct a donkey with a bridle, and lead a rebellious fool with a beating on his backside! Don't respond to the words of a fool with more foolish words, or you will become as foolish as he is! Instead, if you're asked a silly question, answer it with words of wisdom so the fool doesn't think he's so clever.

If you choose a fool to represent you, you're asking for trouble. It will be as bad for you as cutting off your own feet! You can never trust the words of a fool, just like a crippled man can't trust his legs to support him. Give honor to a fool and watch it backfire—like a stone tied to a slingshot. The statements of a fool will hurt others like a thorn bush brandished by a drunk. Like a reckless archer shooting arrows at random is the impatient employer who hires just any fool who comes along—someone's going to get hurt! Fools are famous for repeating their errors, like dogs are known to return to their vomit.

There's only one thing worse than a fool, and that's the smug, conceited man always in love with his own opinions. The lazy loafer says, "I can't go out and look for a job—there may be a lion out there roaming wild in the streets!" As a door is hinged to the wall, so the lazy man keeps turning over, hinged to his bed! There are some people so lazy they won't even work to feed themselves. A self-righteous person is convinced he's smarter than seven wise counselors who tell him the truth. It's better to grab a stray dog by its ears than to meddle in a quarrel that's none of your business. The one who is caught lying to his friend, who says, "I didn't mean it, I was only joking," can be compared to a madman randomly shooting off deadly weapons.

Declarations

- There is way an underserved curse can harm me because it it will find no resting place.
- I depend on the Holy Spirit to turn me from foolishness.
- I walk by the Spirit's leading in the wisdom way.
- I am sensible and hard working.
- I do not take up someone else's offense.
- I do not get involved in an argument that doesn't belong to me.
- I walk in integrity and honesty.
- I say what I do and do what I say, living and working as unto the Lord.

My Personal Revelation of Wisdom

_____

_____

_____

_____

_____

My Personal Applications

_____

_____

_____

_____

_____

_____

My Personal Declarations

_____

_____

_____

_____

_____

_____

"Tolerate the weaknesses of those in the family of faith, forgiving one another in the same way you have been graciously forgiven by Jesus Christ. If you find fault with someone, release this same gift of forgiveness to them"
(Colossians 3:13, TPT).

PROVERBS 27

Here is some random trivia for you. The Bible mentions "gratitude" 157 times and "thanks" or "thanksgiving" 72 times for a total of 229 times between the two words. We can therefore conclude that living with hearts of gratitude and thanksgiving to the Lord and expressing it to Him must be important for them to be talked about so often.

According to Psalms 100:4, thanks is the key to entering his gates. "Enter His gates with thanksgiving, and into His courts with praise. Be thankful to Him and bless His name." Think about this; we have the key to get into His presence wherever we are! Living with a grateful attitude enhances our perspective as we acknowledge Jesus as provider of everything. This simple step has the power to change our lives.

****

Proverbs 27:1-13 – Never brag about the plans you have for tomorrow, for you don't have a clue what tomorrow may bring to you. Let someone else honor you for your accomplishments, for self-praise is never appropriate. It's easier to carry a heavy boulder and a ton of sand than to be provoked by a fool and have to carry that burden! The rage and anger of others can be overwhelming, but it's nothing compared to jealousy's fire. It's better to be corrected openly if it stems from hidden love. You can trust a friend who wounds you with his honesty, but your enemy's pretended flattery comes from insincerity.

When your soul is full, you turn down even the sweetest honey. But when your soul is starving, every bitter thing becomes sweet. Like a bird that has fallen from its nest is the one who is dislodged from his home. Sweet friendships refresh the soul and awaken our hearts with joy, for good friends are like the anointing oil that yields the fragrant incense *of God's presence*. So never give up on a friend or abandon a friend of your father—for in the day of your brokenness you won't have to run to a relative for help. A friend nearby is better than a relative far away.

My son, when you walk in wisdom, my heart is filled with gladness, for the way you live is proof that I've not taught you in vain. A wise, shrewd person discerns the danger ahead and prepares himself, but the naïve simpleton never looks ahead and suffers the consequences. Cosign for one you barely know and you will pay a great price! Anyone stupid enough to guarantee the loan of another deserves to have his property seized in payment.

****

Proverbs 27:17-19 – It takes a grinding wheel to sharpen a blade, and so one person sharpens the character of another. Tend an orchard and you'll have fruit to eat. Serve the Master's interests and you'll receive honor that's sweet. Just as no two faces are exactly alike, so every heart is different.

****

Proverbs 27:24-27 – A man's strength, power, and riches will one day fade away; not even nations endure forever. Take care of your responsibilities and be diligent in your business and you will have more than enough—an abundance of food, clothing, and plenty for your household.

Declarations

- I am thankful for today and live fully present in it.
- I walk in humility and grace in my relationships with others.
- I am thankful for my friends and my family.
- Every day I speak truth with love and thus I am sharpened.
- My heart reflects the real me and I let me show.
- I am a good steward; everything that I have is from the Lord and He trusts me to take care of it.
- Money management is important to God. I manage all that He is entrusting me with.
- God is my source and my provider.

My Personal Revelation of Wisdom

_____

_____

_____

_____

_____

_____

My Personal Applications

_____

_____

_____

_____

_____

_____

My Personal Declarations

_____

_____

_____

_____

_____

"Rejoice always and delight in your faith; be unceasing and persistent in prayer; in every situation [no matter what the circumstances] be thankful and continually give thanks to God; for this is the will of God for you in Christ Jesus. Do not quench [subdue, or be unresponsive to the working and guidance of] the [Holy] Spirit" (1 Thessalonians 5:16-19, AMP).

PROVERBS 28

According to *Thayer's Greek Lexicon,* repentance (metanoia) means to change one's mind. Repentance isn't a one-and-done thing. Repentance should be occurring as we are growing in our relationship with the Lord. This is why the power of the Word and the work of the Holy Spirit in our lives is so important as our anchor.

They help us to divide between our soul and our spirit, eliminating things that are not beneficial and acquiring new ways of thinking that line up with the Word of God. How refreshing it is to know that God through Jesus and the work of the Holy Spirit empowers us to think differently. We can continually learn to have the same mind as Jesus as we progressively grow to know Him more.

****

Proverbs 28:1-9 – Guilty criminals experience paranoia even though no one threatens them. But the innocent lovers of God, because of righteousness, will have the boldness of a young, ferocious lion! A rebellious nation is thrown into chaos, but leaders anointed with wisdom will restore law and order. When a pauper oppresses the destitute, it's like a flash flood that sweeps away their last hope. Those who turn their backs on what they know is right will no longer be able to tell right from wrong. But those who love the truth strengthen their souls.

Justice never makes sense to men devoted to darkness, but those tenderly devoted to the Lord can understand justice perfectly. It's more respectable to be poor and pure than rich and perverse. To be obedient to what you've been taught proves you're an honorable child, but to socialize with the lawless brings shame to your parents. Go ahead and get rich on the backs of the poor, but all the wealth you gather will one day be given to those who are kind to the needy. If you close your heart and refuse to listen to God's instruction, even your prayer will be despised.

Proverbs 28:13-15 – If you cover up your sin you'll never do well. But if you confess your sins and forsake them, you will be kissed by mercy. Overjoyed is the one who with tender heart trembles before God, but the stubborn, unyielding heart will experience even greater evil. Ruthless rulers can only be compared to raging lions and roaming bears.

****

Proverbs 28:18-20 – The pure will be rescued from failure, but the perverse will suddenly fall into ruin. Work hard and you'll have all you desire, but chase a fantasy and you could end up with nothing. Life's blessings drench the honest and faithful person, but punishment rains down upon the greedy and dishonest.

****

Proverbs 28:25-27 – To make rash, hasty decisions shows that you are not trusting the Lord. But when you rely totally on God, you will still act carefully and prudently. Self-confident know-it-alls will prove to be fools. But when you lean on the wisdom from above, you will have a way to escape the troubles of your own making. You will never go without if you give to the poor. But if you're heartless, stingy, and selfish, you invite curses upon yourself.

Declarations

- Confessing and turning away from my sin produces mercy, joy, peace, and a happy life.
- I make repentance a priority and a good habit.
- I am planted firmly in Jesus and depend on His faithfulness to live my faith-filled life.
- I am dependable and can be counted on.
- I trust in the Lord and see beyond myself and my circumstance to help someone in need.

My Personal Revelation of Wisdom

_____

_____

_____

_____

_____

My Personal Applications

_____

_____

_____

_____

_____

My Personal Declarations

_____

_____

_____

_____

_____

"Since these virtues are already planted
deep within, and you possess them in
abundant supply, they will keep you from
being inactive or fruitless in your pursuit
of knowing Jesus Christ more intimately"
(2 Peter 1:8).

PROVERBS 29

Comparison is the thief of joy. It's easy to fall into the habit of looking at what someone else is saying and doing to be the standard for what we should say and do. This is not God's intention. We are each uniquely and wonderfully made and thus there are not two people who are the same.

Our son-in-law is an identical twin and where there is obvious resemblance between the two there are also stark differences in personality, dreams, and goals – along with a slight difference in their eyes. My point is that each of us are unique and each of us are wonderfully made. Let's not expect everyone to think the same or talk the same. Instead let's welcome the differences between people and see that as part of God's plan for the diversity among His creation. Our creative God has purpose and plans for each of us and His heart is for us to lean into our divine purpose and be the best at what only we can do.

****

Proverbs 29:1 – Stubborn people who repeatedly refuse to accept correction will suddenly be broken and never recover.

****

Proverbs 29:7-11 – God's righteous people will pour themselves out for the poor, but the ungodly make no attempt to understand or help the needy. Arrogant cynics love to pick fights, but the humble and wise love to pursue peace. There's no use arguing with a fool, for his ranting and raving prevent you from making a case and settling the argument in a calm way. Violent men hate those with integrity, but the lovers of God esteem those who are holy. You can recognize fools by the way they give full vent to their rage and let their words fly! But the wise bite their tongues and hold back all they could say.

****

Proverbs 29:20 – There's only one kind of person who is

worse than a fool: the impetuous one who speaks without thinking first.

****

Proverbs 29:23-27 – Lift yourself up with pride and you will soon be brought low, but a meek and humble spirit will add to your honor. You are your own worst enemy when you partner with a thief, for a curse of guilt will come upon you when you fail to report a crime. Fear and intimidation is a trap that holds you back. But when you place your confidence in the Lord, you will be seated in the high place. Everyone curries favor with leaders. But God is the judge, and justice comes from him. The wicked hate those who live a godly life, but the righteous hate injustice wherever it's found.

Declarations

- Humility is my way forward.
- With the help of the Holy Spirit I am slow to speak and quick to hear.
- I am becoming a better listener every day. I have no need to vent, but freely share my feelings and/or opinions.
- God's got me, He knows me and my heart.
- In guarding my words carefully, I am trusting Him and bringing Him glory.
- I trust the Lord and live in safety.
- I am free from the fear of man and also from what anyone says or thinks about me.
- I live for God's approval.
- I live to honor God and represent Him well.

My Personal Revelation of Wisdom

_____

_____

_____

_____

_____

_____

My Personal Applications

_____

_____

_____

_____

_____

_____

Wisdom Declarations

My Personal Declarations

_____

_____

_____

_____

_____

"If you bow low in God's awesome presence, he will eventually exalt you as you leave the timing in his hands" (1 Peter 5:6).

"And consider the example that Jesus, the Anointed One, has set before us. Let his mindset become your motivation" (Philippians 2:5).

PROVERBS 30

Have you heard the saying, "You don't know what you don't know?" This truth has the potential to change your life. Let's take a minute and think about this. It seems logical that what you don't know yet, you obviously don't know. Then why do you feel pressure to act as if you do? There is nothing wrong with not knowing, but this can be harmful when you don't want to know or you act like you do know when you don't. There is also harm in feeling as if you must always have to understand why something has happened.

Trust is the remedy to our why; trusting Him with it all and not having to understand but acknowledge Him while watching Him direct our path. Remember that humility is always your way forward. Having a heart and mindset to learn is what Jesus talked about when He said that you must be like a little child to enter into the Kingdom. Being excited and expectant to learn are also characteristics of being like a little child. You truly don't know what you don't know so let's approach each day ready and expectant to learn something new.

****

Proverbs 30:4-9 – Who is it that travels back and forth from the heavenly realm to the earth? Who controls the wind as it blows and holds it in his fists? Who tucks the rain into the cloak of his clouds? Who stretches out the skyline from one vista to the other? What is his name? And what is the name of his Son? Who can tell me? Every promise from the faithful God is pure and proves to be true. He is a wraparound shield of protection for all his lovers who run to hide in him. Never add to his words, or he will have to rebuke you and prove that you're a liar.

God, there are two things I'm asking you for before I die, only two: Empty out of my heart everything that is false—every lie, and every crooked thing. And give me neither undue poverty nor undue wealth—but rather, feed my soul with the measure of prosperity that pleases you. May my satisfaction be found in you. Don't let me be so rich that I don't need you or so poor that I have to resort to dishonesty just to make ends meet. Then my life will never detract from bringing glory to your name.

****

Proverbs 30:18-20 – There are four marvelous mysteries that are too amazing to unravel—who could fully explain them? The way an eagle flies in the sky, the way a snake glides on a boulder, the path of a ship as it passes through the sea, and the way a bridegroom falls in love with his bride. 20Here is the deceptive way of the adulterous woman: she takes what she wants and then says, "I've done nothing wrong."

****

Proverbs 30:24-33 – The earth has four creatures that are very small but very wise: The feeble ant has little strength, yet look how it diligently gathers its food in the summer to last throughout the winter. The delicate rock-badger isn't all that strong, yet look how it makes a secure home, nestled in the rocks. The locusts have no king to lead them, yet they cooperate as they move forward by bands. And the small lizard is easy to catch as it clings to the walls with its hands, yet it can be found inside a king's palace.

There are four stately monarchs who are impressive to watch as they go forth: the lion, the king of the jungle, who is afraid of no one, the rooster strutting boldly among the hens, the male goat out in front leading the herd, and a king leading his regal procession. If you've acted foolishly by drawing attention to yourself, or if you've thought about saying something stupid, you'd better shut your mouth. For such stupidity may give you a bloody nose! Stirring up an argument only leads to an angry confrontation.

Declarations

- In all my questions, the things I don't know, and my lack of understanding I know this: Every word of God is pure and true.
- God is my shield and I put my trust in Him.
- I trust God and I live by His Word.
- Everything I have, God has blessed me with.
- I show my gratitude to Him by stewarding my life well.
- I am a forever learner.
- I learn from the little things, the majestic things, and the everyday things.
- Thank you, Father, for taking such great care of me. You are good and faithful! I love You, Lord.

My Personal Revelation of Wisdom

_____

_____

_____

_____

_____

My Personal Applications

_____

_____

_____

_____

_____

_____

My Personal Declarations

_____

_____

_____

_____

_____

_____

"For every word Yahweh speaks is sure and reliable. His truth is tested, found to be flawless, and ever faithful. It's as pure as silver refined seven times in a crucible of clay" Psalms 12:6).

PROVERBS 31

Mark 12:30 states, "And you must love the Lord your God with all your heart, all your soul, all your mind and all your strength." This was Jesus' response to being asked what is the most important commandment. He continued to say that the second is to love your neighbor as yourself. Here we see that Jesus was clearly saying this is a command, not an option, so we must consider that there is something very important about where our love goes and what we are loving God with.

Loving God with **all** is crucial to our spiritual formation. I want us to consider that loving God with all of our strength involves our abilities, our unique gifting, and our personalities. Whatever we are gifted in and wherever we have ability to do, God wants us to love him with **all** of it. This changes the game to know that God wants you to partner with him in your everyday abilities. His commandment to love Him pretty much covers your whole being and day-to-day life. He goes on to say that it is also important for you to love others well. Living in this type of love with God and others is paramount to developing your new nature in Christ.

****

Proverbs 31:3-4 – So keep yourself sexually pure from the promiscuous, wayward woman. Don't waste the strength of your anointing on those who ruin kings—you'll live to regret it! For you are a king, Lemuel, and it's never fitting for a king to be drunk on wine or for rulers to crave alcohol.

****

Proverbs 31:8-31 – But you are to be a king who speaks up on behalf of the disenfranchised and pleads for the legal rights of the defenseless and those who are dying. Be a righteous king, judging on behalf of the poor and interceding for those most in need. Who could ever find a wife like this one—she is a woman of strength and mighty valor! She's full of wealth and wisdom. The price paid for her was greater than many jewels. Her husband has entrusted his heart to her, for she brings him the rich spoils of victory. All throughout her life she brings him what is good and not evil. She searches out continually to possess that which is pure and righteous. She delights in the work of her hands.

She gives out revelation-truth to feed others. She is like a trading ship bringing divine supplies from the merchant. Even in the night season she arises and sets food on the table for hungry ones in her house and for others. She sets her heart upon a field and takes it as her own. She labors there to plant the living vines. She wraps herself in strength, might, and power in all her works.She tastes and experiences a better substance, and her shining light will not be extinguished, no matter how dark the night. She stretches out her hands to help the needy and she lays hold of the wheels of government.

She is known by her extravagant generosity to the poor, for she always reaches out her hands to those in need. She is not afraid of tribulation, for all her household is covered in the dual garments of righteousness and grace. Her clothing is beautifully knit together—a purple gown of exquisite linen. Her husband is famous and admired by all, sitting as the venerable judge of his people. Even her works of righteousness she does for the benefit of her enemies. Bold power and glorious majesty are wrapped around her as she laughs with joy over the latter days.

Her teachings are filled with wisdom and kindness as loving instruction pours from her lips. She watches over the ways of her household and meets every need they have. Her sons and daughters arise in one accord to extol her virtues, and her husband arises to speak of her in glowing terms. "There are many valiant and noble ones, but you have ascended above them all!" Charm can be misleading, and beauty is vain and so quickly fades, but this virtuous woman lives in the wonder, awe, and fear of the Lord. She will be praised *throughout eternity*. So go ahead and give her the credit that is due, for she has become a radiant woman, and all her loving works of righteousness deserve to be admired at the gateways of every city!

Declarations

- My strength is valuable so I do not waste it on trivial matters.
- I speak up for those in need.
- I am intentionally developing my new nature and growing up in Christ.
- With the help of the Holy Spirit, I identify distractions that are holding me back.
- I abandon those distractions so I can grow into all that He has purposed for me to be.
- I value others for who they are without stumbling over who they are not.

My Personal Revelation of Wisdom

_____

_____

_____

_____

_____

_____

My Personal Applications

_____

_____

_____

_____

_____

_____

My Personal Declarations

_____

_____

_____

_____

_____

"True spirituality that is pure in the eyes of our Father God is to make a difference in the lives of the orphans, and widows in their troubles, and to refuse to be corrupted by the world's values" (James 1:27).

About The Author

Tami Miller loves Jesus and loves people. She has been married to the love of her life, Ted, for twenty-nine years and lives in Arlington, TX. She has raised three wonderful children and has an awesome son-in-law who all make her proud to be their mom! Tami and Ted were lead pastors for twenty-five years and now lead their non-profit ministry Centered Life International. She finds joy in speaking, teaching, writing, and relational learning. Currently, God has directed the Millers to direct their calling to the marketplace where they now serve pastors nationally and globally. Tami always enjoys friends, walks, music, shopping and a great piece of chocolate.

You can email Tami at: tamidmiller3@gmail.com

Tami posts weekly on Instagram and Facebook.
You can find her at:

https://instagram.com/tami.miller3

or

https://www.facebook.com/tami.miller.58511

You can also find her at:
https://www.facebook.com/CenteredLifeInternational/

https://www.inthecenter.life

Made in the USA
Columbia, SC
01 March 2024

32488607R00078